Out of the Habit

Shirley McCann

Cover Photo:

Shirley McCann, age 17, following her installation as a
novice at the Milwaukee Motherhouse. August 4, 1943.

Preface

When I asked myself why I wrote this story, two reasons came to mind. I knew my children had heard bits and pieces of my story over the years, but I wanted my grandchildren and even great grandchildren to know about my stay in the convent.

Secondly, I felt it important to open the doors to a life that is no more. Since the early 1960s, those who choose a religious life have a different preparatory experience than I. Admittance to the Orders of today, especially teaching Orders, is open to women who have already acquired a college degree. Back in the 40s, the greater percentage of applicants entered after high school graduation.

Those following a religious calling no longer live in seclusion from the outside world. The nuns of today live in their own apartments in small groups and are not required to wear the habit. They are free to enter retail establishments and visit their family and friends.

I loved the life, Holy Rule, and even the restrictions under which we lived. I respected the vows taken. If it had not been for one particular experience, I believe I would still be a member of the School Sisters of Notre Dame today.

The way my life has unfolded is a confirmation to me that 1951 was the right time in my life to re-enter the secular world. I will always be grateful for the time spent in the convent because this experience made me the woman I am today.

Chapter One

Early night prayer was finished. Some of the participants had left. I turned once more to view the altar where I had worshiped during the past seven years. It was time for me to return to my cell, the word used in monastic life for bedroom. Somehow I wanted to make the familiar walk along the corridor and up the stairs take longer than it did. There was no urgency in my step. I wanted to remember every moment.

Excitement and some apprehension came over me as I entered my little room for the last time. I checked the drawers of the dresser for anything personal; already knowing nothing there really belonged to me. Everything had been given to me to use. Nothing was mine.

Unpinning the stiffly starched veil, I laid it on my bed parallel to the pillow. It served as a sanctuary that allowed me to see only straight ahead. The veil had become a shield of protection from many distractions.

Memories ran through my mind of the first time this veil was placed on my head. That day was the culmination of a dream come true.

I had grown up believing I was inept at learning and felt I didn't fit in my family. My parents cared for me. Food was always plentiful and our house spotlessly clean, but my world was void of tenderness, encouragement and communication. At age 16, I had found my place in the convent.

Slowly I untied the two pieces of the white wimple covering my head leaving only my face exposed. I lingered to absorb as much of the scent of starch and to feel just the right amount of stiffness in the material, making it possible to form the curved indentation made from shoulder to shoulder. I placed both pieces next to the veil on the bed.

As I lowered my left hand to my side, I felt the beads, chain and cross of the rosary that jingled at my side as I walked. It was a fifteen-decade rosary from which hung a beautiful five-inch crucifix. I had dreamed for years of wearing it, and now I hesitated to leave it behind.

Leaving.

That's what I was doing. Leaving my life-long dream of being a bride of Christ as a nun. The day I made my first communion left a lasting imprint on my mind. I can see myself kneeling in thanksgiving in one of the front pews of Holy Angels Church after receiving the blessed wafer. It felt as if I were being given permission to spend my life for God. The seed had been planted in me at age seven and my commitment was firm by age 13.

When I was 13, an elderly uncle of mine died. Uncle Albert was an uneducated man who did the gardening at our home. Some people looked at him as a man not mentally swift, but I saw him as the kindest, sweetest man I knew. I saw his reverence for the grass, trees, vegetables and flowers. He had such a gentle, fun-loving way with the little critters that showed themselves on the land. But most of all, he was always very good to me. I felt as if he understood the sadness that filled my heart as a child. That feeling as if I didn't belong to the family. I came to believe later, the feeling was in fact a longing for the convent.

Uncle Albert always talked to me about finding the "sugars" in life. When I flew high on my swing, Uncle Albert told me that the breeze I felt was a sugar hug from God. Accepting Uncle's death and my loss affirmed my earlier commitment. It was then that I told my parents that in a few years I would go to the convent. I know they thought it was just a passing fancy, but it was real to me.

My joining and leaving the convent occurred prior to the early 1960s, when priests and nuns shed their garb and habits to work and live among those they served. At the time I left the convent, leaving was a rare event that carried a stigma of scandal. Often the reason for leaving was that they had found comfort in relationships outside the convent. It was rumored that many chose undesirable habits and unhappy lives. Frequently, the men and women who left religious life turned away from God. Leaving the convent when I did met with raised eyebrows and great suspicion. The question was, "What did she do? Whom did she get mixed up with?"

In December 1941, during the middle of my junior year in high school, the call to follow my passion was very strong. A sister at my high school had taken an interest in me. I shared with her my desire to be a nun.

Although I thought I wasn't smart enough to teach as sister did, I figured there would be a role for me in the convent. Though I wouldn't be sixteen for another month, I knew that all I wanted was to live my life for God. After school and some Saturdays while visiting with her, Sister taught me advanced math. I saw she was determined to prove to me that I could learn anything I wanted.

It was then I knew in my heart that it was time for me to leave for the convent. My parents were totally opposed at the thought of it. My mother's big concern was that she was afraid our relatives would laugh when they heard. They might have expected one of my "well behaved" sisters to enter a convent, but I was the last person they envisioned living a disciplined life.

The relatives had seen me climbing trees and fighting with the neighbor boy too often. It was no secret I was not a scholar. Shirley was the noisy attention seeker, the mischievous one of the family. I overheard an old aunt comment to my mother, "Just wait, there will be two pair of shoes under her bed some day." My mother was appropriately upset, but in my naivety, I didn't have any idea what she meant.

My dad just kept saying, "Don't leave us." His decision was a definite "no" until our pastor convinced my father.

He said, "Adolph, let that girl go."

That's all it took. I tried to ignore my mother's tears and my dad's sadness. I felt they eventually would be proud to have a nun for a daughter. I knew my two sisters and their families would take good care of my parents.

The high school Sister who befriended me helped fill out an application. She enclosed a letter of recommendation and a brief note I wrote asking admittance to the candidature. Sister had explained to me that there probably would be several years of probation prior to my being allowed to join the Order. Within a week, a letter of acceptance arrived at our house. I was instructed to make an appointment with a specific physician as soon as possible.

My mother accompanied me to the doctor for the required physical examination to prove I was in good health and a virgin. How I wish my mother had warned me about the type of examination I had. Not understanding what was taking place was traumatic for me. When we left the doctor's office, he gave me a sealed business envelope and told me to give it to the person in charge at the convent.

About two weeks before I left, I had to find my own way downtown to the Motherhouse to be fitted for a candidate's garb. While riding on the bus I tried to imagine what would take place. Previously I had only seen that huge city block structure from the outside. I knew the Motherhouse was the only home in the United States for girls aspiring to join that particular Order. Retired teaching nuns lived there and worked around the Motherhouse for their keep. The high school Sister had told me there were also offices for the nuns who ran the Order.

It took me a couple minutes to work up the courage to knock on the door. I didn't know if I should just tap a bit or pound on it because the door looked so big and heavy. I couldn't find a doorbell or knocker. I'm not sure what I did, but a sister, called the portress, whose everyday job was to tend the door, opened it and motioned me to step in. Without a smile or greeting, she directed me into a little parlor that had a table and a few chairs. As she left the room, she said she would bring someone to see me.

Before long, a little nun carrying a tape measure and note pad bustled in with a smile. Though she seemed pleasant, she never asked my name or commented on my coming to live there. I had to twist and turn as she swung the tape measure around. Within a few minutes she filled several pages of her notebook. I had to take off a shoe to get my foot measurement also. With that, she spun around and hurriedly left the room. I didn't know what to do.

Was I to walk out or wait for the portress to show me out? I just walked out. When I found myself back on the street, I became aware that almost no words had been exchanged. I wondered if I had done something wrong.

When I arrived home, my mother didn't feel like talking, so I went over to my sister's house. After telling her about my experience, she covered my concern by saying that nuns don't talk a lot. Somehow that comment seemed to satisfy me.

Mid-January, a postcard came from the Motherhouse stating I was to present myself the following week at 4:00 p.m. On January 21, 1942, just five weeks before my sixteenth birthday, with nothing in hand, my parents and I presented ourselves at the door of the Motherhouse. The portress closed the door as an elderly nun greeted us and ushered us into a small parlor. After exchanging a few pleasantries, Sister said someone would join us shortly.

A jovial middle-aged nun entered the room and introduced herself as the Candidates' Mistress. I understood from what she said that I would have to answer to her for everything until I was accepted into the Order. It was a relief to see her smile and even joke a bit. There was kindness in her eyes and tone of voice.

Sister sent me off with another nun to change clothes. The room we entered must have been the sewing room. Several nuns were sewing at machines and a group of candidates sat around doing some hand sewing. No one was talking, but everyone seemed happy. It took only a few minutes to change into my new clothes. When I was dressed, the helping sister put my street clothes and shoes in a paper bag. My parents seemed surprised when I returned dressed as a candidate. I felt very grown up in the long, black, belted serge dress and black cape that covered the upper part of my body.

A few minutes after I returned to the room, the Candidate's Mistress suggested it was time for my parents to leave. I remember my mother slowly going through the motions of picking up her purse after she had buttoned her coat. Dad had my coat and was going to hand it to me. I saw tears in his eyes.

He said, "Here, you'll need this."

The Candidate's Mistress smiled and said, "No, she'll be fine without it."

There was a strained feeling in the room. The nun who had helped me dress handed my father the bag of my street clothes. After a brief hug and kiss, my parents were on their way.

When I think about it, I don't know why it didn't bother me when my parents left. I knew they would miss me. I don't think it occurred to me that I might miss them. I knew my life would be different and no matter what it would be like, I knew it was the life for me. I had made this choice of my own free will.

Chapter Two

The Candidates' Mistress had a gentle way about herself. I felt comfortable being with her. She welcomed me and explained that the candidature would give me a feel of what community living would be like. Sister said the sooner I set aside the memories of living a secular life, the sooner I would find pleasure and contentment in my new surroundings.

I hadn't been told this before but Sister ended our little chat by saying that within an hour, a seven-day retreat would begin. She said it would be a silent retreat, but because I was new, a candidate would be appointed to whisper answers to my pressing questions. She went on to explain that although we do not raise our eyes to catch another's eyes, I had permission to look around in order to find the other candidate.

The days sped by and somehow those seven days were very easy for me. I was awe-struck that a whole church was contained in this building, as well as a magnificent perpetual adoration chapel. At all hours we could hear beautiful chanting. Those soft melodious sounds made me think of heaven.

We had prayer time, quiet time and time for singing. A priest gave us inspiring talks. It was the first time in my life I was really alone within myself. Even when we gathered in the refectory for our meals, there wasn't a clink or clang from silverware against a plate or bowl. Later I found out the noise would not be respectful to the person doing the spiritual reading as we ate. I had never been exposed to such beautiful peace. Even though I am a talkative person, the silence was very soothing. It is difficult to explain, but I felt as if I had come home.

My biggest challenge during the retreat was to keep from stumbling up the high stairways or falling down them. For the first couple days, I looked as if I were an actress in a comedic skit. My awkwardness was getting the best of me. My problem wasn't trying not to catch anyone's eye, but rather how to figure out what the others were doing that made it easy for them to go up and down the stairs. It helped that there were railings to cling to, because I was either stepping on the front of the dress or catching my heel in the back. It took a while until I caught on to the easy maneuver of lifting the front of the dress slightly when ascending stairs. With a little practice, I was able to reach behind me and gently lift a little fold of material in the back that cleared the heels.

It was later that I learned how to walk in order to appear as if I were gliding across the floor. Come to think of it, nuns always looked as if they were being carried along a moving walkway. The trick was to take very small lady-like steps. It took practice to take those steps quickly enough to cover territory and still hold the head and spine erect. The other candidates had mastered this already.

I frequently heard the Candidate's Mistress repeating, "Quickly now, head and spine erect" or "Little steps, little steps."

Because of the many corridors and walkways, called arcades, it was very easy to get lost. One particular time when I turned left instead of right, I found myself walking in the midst of a group of sisters. I don't know where they were headed, but I knew I wasn't supposed to be there.

One of the sisters pulled me aside to redirect me, but only after she informed me that candidates have no business intruding on the professed nuns. Sister didn't know I was new, but chastised me because that area was a sanctuary safe from intruders. She told me it was her duty to report me, but I didn't care because I knew the Candidate's Mistress would understand.

At night we climbed the stairs to our dormitory on the fifth floor of the building. We each had our little curtained section consisting of a small bed and nightstand. Besides the two deep drawers that held extra underclothes, the nightstand had a towel rack fastened to the side. Each week we were given a fresh towel and washcloth.

On retiring, we took our large bowl and glass to the one sink on the floor to get water for the next morning to wash up and brush our teeth. The homemade soap we used was not perfume-scented. Our toiletries consisted of a comb, brush, toothbrush and a small container with baking soda for brushing our teeth. The entire three and a half years I spent in the Motherhouse, I never saw a mirror.

During the winter it would sometimes get so cold in the dorm that the water in our bowls would be frozen in the morning. I remember using the end of my toothbrush to chip through the ice. We all moved quickly to get ourselves ready and down the stairs to the Chapel for morning prayer.

In contrast, we welcomed the breezes of summer by opening many windows. The Mistress said there were no screens because we were so high up that the flies and mosquitoes wouldn't bother us. We found out flies and mosquitoes have no boundaries. I wasn't peppered with bites, but I did shoo them from my cubicle, hoping they might find someone else to bother.

Our regular routine called for discipline, silence and structure. I felt sorry for some of the girls who had entered the previous fall. Quite a few were still crying themselves to sleep at night because of homesickness. I wondered why this way of life was so easy for me. It was as if I had lived like this before.

After the retreat it was fun meeting the other candidates during our one hour of recreation following lunch and dinner. There was a spacious courtyard for us to gather and play games. It was fun playing baseball in the courtyard that was big enough for a good size diamond. We made quite a spectacle when we jumped rope or played tag. The first thing to learn was not to lift the long skirt, but hold it close to us. During the winter it was mostly snowball fights and just running around to stay warm. We wore a white scarf over our heads and a long black cape to keep us warm.

Normally we wore nothing on our heads except when we went into chapel. Those were the days when no woman or girl entered a Catholic church without some covering on her head. When I was growing up, a handkerchief and a bobby pin often took the place of a hat or scarf.

For chapel we wore a bonnet that reminded me of the one my mother wore when she did her gardening. I always thought that hers was similar to those the frontier women wore. The only real difference was that this bonnet was completely white and starched firmly. It tied under the chin and when the strings were drawn, the back of the bonnet would respond in pleats. The starched sides rested on our cheeks. It came forward so far that it blocked all peripheral vision, intended to minimize distractions and to help us focus on God. The lower half of the pleats rested on the tops of our shoulders. No matter what went on behind us, we couldn't possibly turn our head without turning our whole bodies around. From the back, we created a sea of white heads, so still and disciplined, whether we were truly lost in contemplation or not.

The smell of the starch in the bonnet brought about memories of times my mother starched doilies and my dad's shirts. I wondered if the laundry sisters had it as easy as she, because I learned they used little flatirons heated on top of the stove for all ironing.

I had occasion to go into the laundry room one day when sent on an errand. At least ten sisters were lined up in front of a padded narrow table. Behind them stood a long stove with multiple burners. Many small all metal irons were heated on the burners at one time. When one iron had cooled, the sister turned around and replaced the cool one on the stove. Using the same potholder she had been using, she lifted a new iron to work with. Despite their primitive tools, the sisters' work was flawless.

Chapter Three

Every minute of our candidature days was accounted for. Classes and study time filled seven days a week. During my first three and a half months, I had a private tutor to complete high school. I particularly remember a fair but strict sister who taught English literature and grammar. She was an excellent teacher. We covered that one and a half years' work in ten weeks. I could hardly keep up with the reading. Writing a composition almost every day didn't seem as challenging as having to stand before her and recite a poem or give a talk. It didn't help that I was self-conscious. I think there were remnants in my consciousness from early childhood when I believed I lacked ability to learn.

It was this sister's goal to clear heads of what she called "Milwaukee-eez". It seemed anyone from this area not only had a Midwest accent, but we labeled ourselves from the Milwaukee area by our choice of words and the endings attached to them. A big clue when we wrote or spoke was the use of "anyways" instead of anyway. Sometimes in conversation a "d" took the place of a beginning "th" for instance, "Dey were told to put der shoes on."

Sister said the habit began from the strong German influence in Milwaukee. She broke this habit by making sure I crossed every "t" and dotted every "i" when I spoke. Her training served me well all my life.

I took a battery of tests in math, history, science, grammar and literature when I arrived. The results determined what I had to cover to graduate from high school. There was no ceremony to celebrate the official high school diploma I received. Without a break in the routine, college classes and teacher training started, May 1, 1942. It was a rugged schedule, but I loved it. I know I never worked so hard in my life. It was exciting to realize I could learn and the teachers were pleased with my work.

One day I experienced an embarrassing moment during an ethics class. A priest who authored the textbook was our teacher. Day after day he droned on and on about the wondrousness of his writings and his magnificent textbook. His class was very formal and dull. He addressed us as ladies. I was Lady Shirley. We were told to stand at our desk when we were addressed. During class one day, a student asked him a question. He responded emphatically by saying "Surely".

Still caught in a daydream, I jumped up and in my most interested manner I could assume I said, "Would you repeat the question please?"

There was bedlam. Everyone broke out in laughter except the teacher. He had a frightful look of astonishment on his face. Because he didn't know how to quiet the class, he said, "You're excused." With that he turned and left the room. From that time on, any time a teacher used the word surely, all heads turned my way.

Almost daily during recreation, I noticed an older nun walking with a cane from one of the doorways to a small grotto located in the corner of the courtyard. It was apparent that walking was difficult and she needed more than just the cane for assistance. I was happy to lend an arm. She never spoke except to say thank you. I didn't expect a conversation, because it was my recreational hour and probably not hers. One time when we reached the grotto, she sat on a bench outside, pulled on my sleeve and motioned for me to sit next to her.

The first thing she said was, "Do you know your guardian angel's name?"

I said, "I know I have a guardian angel, but I never knew it had a name."

Sister went on to say that angels would be very important to me in my life and that I should be better acquainted with my guardian angel.

She said, "As you rest your head on the pillow tonight, quiet yourself, close your eyes and ask your angel to give you its name. The very first name that pops into your mind is your angel's name. Thank the angel and never forget that name."

With that she sort of pushed me aside and said, "Go play." I stood and watched her rise slowly and step into the grotto.

This experience was on my mind all day. That evening I followed her directions and reverently asked my angel its name. To my surprise, immediately the name Celeste came to me. Even though I can't say for sure my angel's name is Celeste, I do know I've been closer to her by being able to address her by name. During recreation I kept helping sister when I saw her in the courtyard, but she never spoke to me again except for "thank you".

As candidates we served as errand runners around the Motherhouse. My favorite errand was to be sent to the tapestry room where gorgeous vestments were made for the priests to be used when they officiated at Mass and ceremonies. These garments were not just for our two chaplains, but also for orders coming from all over the United States.

The colorful brocade fabrics were cut and sewn to size. I saw many nuns reverently hand-embroider spectacular designs on vestments, capes and even altar cloths. I admired the close work and tiny stitches they made. Sewing never was, nor is it now, one of my talents. However, I must admit that when repairing something, I love to do it by hand and make the smallest stitches I can.

The Motherhouse itself had so many mysteries to uncover that it was hard for us not to be curious. Just picture a square city block with five-story buildings around the perimeter. The center area was the courtyard. This Motherhouse was a city unto itself. Besides the church and chapel, it had a barbershop, a library and a sewing room for making our clothes. There was a large kitchen to prepare the meals for several refectories, the convent's mess halls. A large infirmary was well staffed with nuns, who were nurses, to care for ill sisters.

The convent housed a gift shop and a shoe repair shop, and the tapestry room. There was a complete laundry, along with classrooms, meeting rooms, and small dormitories to bed hundreds of nuns.

The dimly lit tunnels in the basement were particularly intriguing. We saw some long corridors marked "Keep Out." Our vivid imaginations conjured up some pretty wild tales. It was easy to pretend there were ghosts or even a hidden treasure waiting behind the twisting halls and closed doors.

Chapter Four

Every so often some of us were called out of study hall for an afternoon. The sisters referred to our assignment as a work project. Some local businesses would reimburse the Motherhouse for our preparing massive mailings. In the early 1940s, there were no machines that did collating of material.

This required our going down to the basement where eight-foot tables were lined up in a row. As a rule, there were about 15 boxes of printed sheets. It wasn't unusual to have some 8000 sheets provided for us to make over a hundred manuals consisting of 70 some pages.

The boxes were opened to find which one had the title page. Gradually the tables were lined with stacks of paper, arranged in numerical sequence. Usually the boxes had sheets with consecutive page numbers, but not always. The line of tables would stretch long enough to accommodate 35 stacks of paper placed on each side.

Then the procession would begin. To keep us from gabbing and probably to stay focused, once we started walking around the tables, we began the recitation of the Rosary.

At times there would be as many as 15 of us walking around the table putting together each unit. It wasn't long before we could hear whispered complaints. "My feet are beginning to hurt." "I'm getting too tired to walk." A few of us spoke up in agreement when we heard, "These stacks don't look any smaller than when we started." The only time comments weren't mixed up with the words of a Hail Mary were when some sister came around to check on us.

When we reached the last page on the table, the packet was placed crosswise against the other on another table. Eventually one or two candidates dropped out of the line to start packing them in a box. The company provided colored pieces of paper to separate the packets in order to use the same boxes again. When the project was complete, the carton boxes were taped shut, ready for the company to pick them up.

Inevitably a few weeks after the first project was returned to the company, those same boxes would be delivered to the Motherhouse again. About 120 booklets would have been bound and this time we were provided with 120 large brown envelopes, labels and postage stamps. At least we were able to sit down for this.

The tables were arranged for piecework. A couple of candidates did the labeling, others stuffed the envelopes, and after the postage was in place, the next group sealed them. The final step was to pack the large 120 prepared envelopes back into the boxes. After they were sealed, the company came and picked them up again. This type of work was tiring, but we were young and didn't mind skipping a study period.

Our daily responsibilities weren't punishment, but we were just the youngest and probably the strongest of all the residents. Periodically it fell to us to scrub the corridors of the arcades on our hands and knees. I was one of the fortunate ones whose pail of water was never accidentally tipped over by a careless or maybe even spiteful sister walking by. In my naivety, I had thought nuns were always special people who only knew kindness and helpfulness. This and similar incidents made me start to realize a religious habit itself didn't change a person on the inside.

We considered ourselves lucky if the work roster directed us to clean several large restrooms. There were more than enough in this five-story facility. Ironically, restroom duty was favored because it was easier than scrubbing arcades on our knees.

Some retired sisters took care of the dusting of the floors and furniture. Two nuns, called sacristans, cared for the altars and vessels in the adoration chapel and the church.

Chapter Five

In August 1942, I was received as a Postulant of the Order, the last step before becoming a part of the sisterhood. I wondered if they had made a mistake because I was much younger than most of the girls who had to wait another year. There were only 18 of us out of the forty-some that had been candidates. There was no formal installation.

One day the Candidate's Mistress summoned us and said we were to remove our things from the candidates' cloakroom. She emphasized that we leave our white bonnets there. As postulants we wore a soft black veil all the time. It covered most of our hair. The veil was attached to a narrow white band that framed our face.

Quite a few of the girls were sent home, because the sisters who were elected to run the Order decided that they would never become nuns. Others had to repeat the year and joined the new group of candidates who

entered the order in August. Our routine as postulants
was similar to what it was before. We shared classes
with the candidates because we were all at different
levels of our studies. Great consideration was given to
the fact that each of us had our strengths and
weaknesses in various subjects. There were many
teachers available to oversee our work. We spent six
days a week in the classroom and studied seven days a
week.

During this time I had to make up a series of
pedagogy classes. I was the only student in the class.
The candidates who entered the previous August
already had finished it. I knew from the start of the
class that I would love being a teacher.

The last class was to be a demonstration session. I
had to choose a subject and write out a detailed lesson
plan. After my teacher approved the plan, the only
thing left to do was to set a date and time. Some
postulants volunteered to be fourth grade students and
an invitation was given to the Candidates Mistress to
attend. All went well, but I realized it took more than
"Open your books to page so and so and start to read."

As Postulants our meals and recreation time were
separate from the candidates. We were told that even
though we participated in classes with them, we could
no longer mingle.

I knew better than to expect much when a big issue
was made of the fact that we were going to have our
own separate dormitory. No matter how good our new
dorm could be, it still meant climbing the stairs to the
fifth floor. We found the square footage was bigger,
but it had the same type of sink, and the size of our
curtained cell was no larger than before.

More was expected of us in the eyes of the Candidates' Mistress. There was now a real possibility of being accepted into the Order. One thing that worked to our advantage was that although we still had daily chores, they were less menial than before. One task I particularly enjoyed was to carry bowls of food from the kitchen to the main refectory where the professed sisters ate. As candidates we had never been allowed to enter that dining area.

As when we were candidates, our parents and family members were able to come to visit every other month for two hours on a Sunday afternoon. Usually my parents and sisters came. My Mother baked a pie or cake, which was taken directly to the kitchen to be shared by all. I could count on my parents to save a sweet treat for me, sometimes a homemade donut or a couple of cookies.

Conversations with my family seemed strained at times, as if there were less and less for us to talk about. I could tell my family didn't want to emphasize any fun or exciting news from home, for fear I might think I was missing something. I know they didn't believe me or understand I was happy. They were surprised to hear that I was studying so much, certainly not a quality of the Shirley they remembered. It was hard to explain to them that I was so excited to find out that I could learn. It was as if a new world were opening up to me.

As a candidate, as well as a postulant, we were allowed to receive mail once a month. I knew I could count on a letter from my Dad. He would try to be funny when relating their daily activities, but somehow I could tell from the choice of his words that he missed me. If an urgent letter arrived that we thought needed a response, we had to ask permission to reply. A denial of permission was considered a good exercise for us in obeying cheerfully. After all, we were preparing to take a vow of obedience. I was very happy and none of the restrictions bothered me.

An uncle passed away and my parents included that news in a letter. When I asked permission to send a note to my Dad to give to the grieving family, I was told to offer prayers for the deceased instead.

Sister said, "Tell your Dad when he visits what you want relayed to your aunt."

Something very interesting took place during this time. One of the English teachers decided to direct a play as a fundraiser for the Motherhouse. None of us had ever heard of this type of a fundraiser before. Normally every other month there would be a big sale in the gift shop of religious items and crafts made by the sisters.

This play was about an ancient queen who ruled her kingdom with an iron hand. I don't recall the story line at all. There were no auditions. One day Sister walked among the candidates and us, the postulants, handing out scripts to quite a few. I was surprised when I saw my copy, because it indicated I was to play Queen Agrippina, wife of Claudius and mother of Nero. At first I was delighted to have been chosen for that part.

When I thanked Sister for choosing me, she was quick to respond, "You're the only one we thought had a strong enough voice to be heard in the back of the hall."

Sister's comment hurt my feelings, because as a youngster, I was convinced I could emulate anyone I saw on the movie screen. Her words made me determined to prove myself.

Rehearsals were great fun because our rigid routine was broken. Memorizing the script was a snap. I was a part of all three acts. There was no change of scenery required because all the acts took place in the throne room of the palace. It felt very strange to be walking around in costumes rather than in my black dress.

In those days there were no microphones or amplifiers available in the Motherhouse. The set was rather primitive. The postulants built the set according to the plans Sister had drawn out. Most fun was being told we could use our creativity in painting and decorating the set.

It was a good thing sister suggested we pick up the hem of our dress and safety pin it behind us at the waist as we worked. It was better that our long slips took the brunt of the mess. It was quite a challenge to remove the glue and paint stains from the slips before putting them in the laundry.

No one minded the fact that we gave up every recreation period working on this. I don't recall whether it took weeks or a month of preparation, but I do know it was great fun and a unique diversion from our normal routine.

There were only two performances. The first one was for all the resident sisters. The second one was on visiting Sunday. All of our families and friends were invited. My parents, sisters and their husbands came. It was the first time that my celebrity brother-in-law, a professional singer, came to the Motherhouse. I so wanted him to be pleased with my performance.

The show went well, without anyone forgetting their lines or props not working. I felt exhilarated bowing before the audience at the end. Having never excelled in anything before this, I ate up every bit of praise given to me that day. I knew my family would say nice things, regardless of how the performance went, but I felt so important because I was complimented by many of the guests.

As I anticipated, my brother-in-law had nothing but praise for my performance. That really made my day.

At Christmastime during my second year, I was permitted to spend two days with my family. That would be the last time I would be in my parents' home be it holiday or not. I was happy to be with my folks and sisters with their families. It was quite a treat to enjoy my Mother's cooking again. There were presents and excitement, but I was eager to return to what I now knew as home.

During the visit, I needed to explain something difficult to my parents. The Order I would be entering was semi-cloistered and under the jurisdiction of the Vatican and not the Bishop.

This Order permitted its professed nuns only one home visit for each of their parents if they became ill. If a visit were granted for a parent and the parent didn't die, no second visit would be allowed at the time of death. I don't recall any objections on my parents' part, yet I believe in my heart that they didn't understand the ramifications.

The law of the Vatican is called Canon Law. It was explained that this law stipulates that semi-cloistered Orders live a more strenuous life than those Orders under the jurisdiction of the Bishops. Our families had to understand the visitation restrictions and also that when a professed nun dies, anything she acquired through inheritance is retained by the Order. Any monetary acquisitions from publications or services rendered automatically became payable to the Order.

Chapter Six

On a Saturday morning in May 1943, a Motherhouse volunteer drove me to a local parish for my one week of required practice teaching. This was a large mission with 12 teachers and a house sister who did the cooking and laundry.

I was greeted at the door and taken to meet with Sister Superior. She explained that one of the parlors was converted into a sleeping room during my stay. She told me I would be addressed as Shirley Ann, because the name Shirley was not a saint's name.

Their school had eight grades. I was assigned to the fifth-grade teacher. She was tall and stately and had a nice smile. Sister talked with her hands a great deal. I saw her catch herself doing that and quickly whip her hands into the wide sleeves of the habit. When the sisters weren't using their hands, they were to keep them hidden in their sleeves.

Sister Superior instructed my mentor to show me where I would sleep, the place I would occupy in the Chapel, the table and chair I could use in the community room, and the sunroom where I would take my meals. The professed sisters were not allowed to eat with a layperson or should I say, I was not allowed to eat with the professed sisters.

Everyone seemed friendly. During silence time I sat at my table and looked through all of the fifth-grade textbooks. At recreation some of the sisters included me with games they were playing. Sunday evening, the sister to whom I had been assigned showed me the lesson plan book for the week.

After that she stood and said, "I'll teach and you observe. As the week progresses, maybe you can give a presentation."

I couldn't wait until Monday morning.

Stepping into the classroom with Sister was so exciting. I felt so grown up. The children looked me over as they came into the room. There were about 40 children in this fifth-grade class. When the bell rang, their moving around and talking came to a stop. They fell into their seats in a flash and all eyes were on sister and me.

I was introduced as Shirley Ann, someone who had come to observe them.

At times I walked around and looked at the work the children were doing, but mostly I observed Sister. The first couple of days, I worked with one of the reading groups, sang songs with the class and actually presented a grammar lesson. I was pretty proud of how everything was going; surely Sister would have to think I'd make a good teacher.

Standing close to the blackboard one day, I made a big mistake. I corrected a spelling error Sister had made on the board. My thought was that I should correct it before one of the students spotted it. After that, everything went downhill fast.

Obviously embarrassed, Sister directed me to a chair and said, "For the rest of the week, you sit there."

I wasn't permitted to observe the children's work anymore, nor did I have an opportunity to present any material to them. The atmosphere in the convent house changed also. No one was rude to me or said anything hurtful, but it was obvious that I was being shunned. Neither Sister Superior nor the teacher gave me any encouragement.

After that, things were tense between Sister and me. She conducted the class as if I were not there. Earlier in the week, she appeared indifferent toward the children, where as now, she was feigning over them to gain their affection.

On one occasion during a history discussion, a student said, "What does Shirley Ann think?" I tried to agree with the teacher's point of view, but no matter what I said, Sister found fault with it.

I have one very pleasant memory of that week. One evening shortly after recreation had started, the doorbell rang. The sister who answered the door came into the community room and said, "We have company. Someone is here to visit us and he knows you, Shirley Ann."

Quite a few of us walked to the main parlor. To my surprise, the visitor was my brother-in-law, John. He had been working in the vicinity and thought he'd stop in on his way home. He had heard I was at that mission. John wasn't Catholic and had no idea there was a protocol to our accepting visitors.

All the sisters were very friendly. I told them that John was a soloist for the Tripoli Chanters of Milwaukee. He was very obliging when someone asked him to sing for us. I requested my favorite, "Because." As a youngster, he and my sister frequently took me for rides on Sunday afternoons. I always coaxed him to sing this song for me. He had a magnificent tenor voice. He concluded that evening by singing the "Lord's Prayer." It made me so proud and pleased because the sisters enjoyed his visit.

On the whole, my recollection of that week is that it was a total disaster. As I look back, I believe I was placed under the tutelage of an insecure teacher. I probably was the first student teacher she worked with.

Feeling discouraged that I would never make it as a teacher, I begged the Candidates' Mistress when I returned to allow me to be what was called a house sister, perhaps a laundress or cook sister. The Motherhouse had a shoe repair shop to care for the nuns' shoes. I was sure I could learn something like that.

I said, "Please, I'll wash clothes, fix shoes or even learn to cook." Sister's sweet pudgy face opened to a broad grin followed by hearty laughter. The Candidates' Mistress assured me that my experience could not have been as bad as hers. She consoled me with stories of how she used to shake and fumble for words whenever she was in front of the students. She actually cried in front of them once. Her words helped restore my confidence.

The Candidates' Mistress most emphatically said, "It's back to the books for you, young lady."

When all the postulants returned from mission, it was fun swapping stories about their week. None of their experiences were very good, but it was the consensus of all that they were grateful not to have been sent to the school I was.

Chapter Seven

In July of 1943, each postulant had to present herself before the Provincial Council to be accepted into the Order as a novice. The Council was composed of Reverend Mother, who was the head of the Order in the United States, and four assistants also elected by the membership.

We eighteen postulants were in a dither. We couldn't eat nor study. The interviews began in the morning. Some of the girls came out crying, saying it was so rough, but they were accepted.

Silence time or not, several of us huddled together to try to figure out what was going to take place when we went into that little room. If tears were being shed, it had to mean those Provincial sisters must have heard things about us. The Candidate's Mistress didn't know everything we did. To this day I can't figure out how they knew things about us that the Candidates' Mistress didn't.

Tension mounted when everything was delayed for lunch. Who would want to eat at a time like this? Why wouldn't those who were already accepted talk about it or at least tell us what they were asked? We agreed this was the longest day we had ever spent. There was no special order in which the girls were called, so we didn't know when our name would come up.

When it was my turn I entered the room, knelt down and in my strongest voice said, "I, Shirley Gerlach, humbly beg for admittance to the Order of School Sisters of Notre Dame."

There were routine questions about my ability to practice the holy vows of poverty, chastity and obedience. Reverend Mother talked about the challenge of living in peace and harmony when sent on mission. The sisters in the parish where I would be sent to teach would be comprised of woman of all ages with their own idiosyncrasies. She stressed that as the youngest, most recently professed, I'd be expected to serve the others willingly and cheerfully. In my mind I compared it to being a freshman in high school. I knew I could handle it.

Someone had to have been keeping very good records over the years because I was questioned about many things I had done since I arrived, including a few innocent indiscretions. It seems some postulants were prone to mischief more than others. I'm not sure if I drifted to them or they to me. Regardless, I was part of a core group who frequently were reprimanded for some escapade or another.

On one occasion while in a restricted corridor of the tunnel, we found a door that needed to be pried open if we were going to check it out. The latch was wobbly and didn't release. We couldn't get it to open. Pulling and prodding didn't do any good, so finally someone ran for a kitchen knife. A couple of pokes and tugs and the door creaked open. We hurried in and the door closed behind us.

The room was rather large, but musty and dark. The one little light that hung from the ceiling was so dim we couldn't make out the labels on any boxes. The few that we opened contained old coats, dresses, shoes, bonnets, and outrageous hats. Some shoes were flat, but others went half way up the calf of the leg. The shoes had some eyelets toward the bottom for a shoestring, but farther up the leg there were just hooks to twist the lace around. Some shoes looked like party slippers.

We wondered who last wore all those shoes.

One girl tried on a pair of pantaloons. She jammed her dress inside them, which made her look three feet wide. She puffed up her cheeks, put her hands over her hair and in a high-pitched voice said, "I vant to be a nun." We laughed so hard as each one of us was sillier than the other.

There was a long coat that had about thirty buttons from the collar all the way down to the hem. It took the girl, who tried it on forever to get the coat closed. We couldn't decide whether the owner of that coat stepped into it already half buttoned or just never buttoned it at all.

Some of the dresses were covered with ruffles and lace. The fabrics were so different than those we were acquainted with. At first we thought these might be costumes someone wore in plays.

A shawl and fancy hat caught my eye. The long shawl had 16 or 18-inch tassels. The fabric was rather

soft and elegant. Someone had added a large section of
ornate embroidery at both ends. We could tell it was
hand embroidered and probably of value. I felt
glamorous wrapping the shawl around me. I picked up
a big hat to complete the ensemble. Holding my nose
in the air and acting as if I were smoking a cigarette, I
pretended to be a high society woman. I couldn't pull
that off with dignity. The tassels from the shawl got
caught in my hands as I was trying to keep the hat on
my head. The brim was so wide; the hat was sliding
from one side to another.

The boxes of hats contained high hats, big hats, and
little ones. Trying them all on made us act up more
than before. There were hats with long feathers
attached with clusters of beads. Some had long colored
ribbons attached to them. Those ribbons were long
enough to make great big bows under the chin. We
found a parasol at the bottom of one box. It was like
stepping back into another era and having great fun
doing it.

We figured these items were probably the street
clothes of early candidates going back almost to the
hundred-year history of the Motherhouse. Our
imaginations were triggered as we wondered what
stories these clothes held. The soil build-up on the
shoes told us they predated sidewalks.

Our fun came to a halt when one of us discovered
the door only opened from the outside. We began to
call out and knock on the door. Some girls began to
cry, while others questioned if anyone would come to
look for us. We really didn't want anyone to find us
there, but we didn't know how to get out.

After some time, an elderly nun opened the door
and reprimanded us not only for being in a restricted

area, but also for the mess that caught her eye. At her direction, we put everything back in the boxes and the boxes back on the shelves. This all would have turned out differently if some sweet understanding sister had opened the door. As it turned out, it was a sister without humor who found us.

Later it didn't help that we got the giggles as we stood in front of the Candidate's Mistress trying to explain how we came upon the room so innocently. It was our perception that she had a hard time keeping a straight face as she imposed a 12-stanza poem to be memorized and recited within 10 days.

Besides enjoying a few of these adventures, it was always fun to play a trick or two on some overly serious postulant. It was easy to hide the book used for table reading and watch the reader enter the refectory and not find it on the lectern. It was hard to keep an innocent look on our faces as she hurried around frantically looking for it. Somehow later in the day, the book would turn up on her desk.

I'm reminded of another foolish thing our little group was involved in. At one end of the Motherhouse complex was a huge bell tower. One of my cohorts discovered a camouflaged door on the third floor that led to a stairway. Of course we had to check it out. We decided to slip out of a study period one by one and meet at the base of the stairs at a designated time. All went according to schedule. There were five of us who began the climb.

It seemed to take forever going up the circular slate stair well. The steps were about three feet wide and wove themselves around a wide pole. We knew the tower was much higher than our fifth floor dormitory, but we had no idea how many steps there were.

After a while, the lead girl called down to us, "There's a platform up here. You're almost there."

Because we had seen a big open area around the bell at the top of the tower, we expected to see a view of the city. As we stood on the platform, it was a disappointment to find, that we were surrounded by a 20 or 30-foot wall extending to the bell tower. A long rope hung from the bell to about three feet from the floor of the platform. The rope reminded me of ropes used on the anchors of big boats.

Because bells were rung often during the day, we thought it would be fun to ring it. That rope was a big temptation for all of us. Who was going to ring the bell? After we pointed our finger at each other saying, "You do it." "You do it." One girl, and I'll never say who, took on the challenge.

At first she tugged and pulled on the rope and nothing happened. That bell was heavier than we thought. Only when she reached up as high as she could on the rope and lifted her feet did the bell begin to ring. The heavy bongs began. As the bell moved from side to side, she swung back and forth. We could tell she was surprised and enjoying it. It looked like fun. The bell rang and rang and rang and she was swinging back and forth.

Our friend would've kept hanging there if someone hadn't shouted, "Let go of the rope! The bell is ringing too much."

Whoever rang the bell regularly probably wore gloves. The palms of the girl's hands were red and sore. The vibratory echo could still be heard and felt when we decided to descend the stairs. We had to hurry before someone checked to see why the bell rang.

We found the Candidate's Mistress waiting for us at the bottom of the stairs. It didn't look good for us. We could tell by Sister's demeanor that we were in for it. Our Mistress had always been so understanding and sweet, but I guess with this we had crossed the line. Without a smile and with her eyes riveted on us, she said, "Why would you do something like this? You know when the Angelus Bell is rung."

One of us said, "We didn't know that was the Angelus bell."

Sister went on to explain that there were three bells on the premises. One bell was rung to alert us and the neighboring community that Mass was about to begin. Another was a tolling bell rung only when someone died in the Motherhouse. The Angelus bell was rung only at 6:00 in the morning, noon and at 6:00 p.m.

We all felt terrible because we never intended to upset Sister.

After Sister reprimanded us, she said to follow her to her office. Once there, she told us our actions were not those of young women preparing to join the sisterhood. When asked, none of us admitted who actually rang the bell. We knew we were in this together.

Sister didn't push the issue. For our punishment, we all had to memorize the 180 lines of Francis Thompson's poem, "The Hound of Heaven." She stated that it could be recited to designated proctors in 60 line segments. To this day, I still remember parts of it.

I fled Him, down the nights and down the days;
I fled Him, down the arches of the years;
I fled Him, down the labyrinthine ways of my own mind;
And in the mist of tears, I hid from Him,..

Our intention was not to disappoint Sister or have her give up on us. When the five of us talked about it later, we were sorry we had disgraced Sister. It probably looked to the other nuns in the Motherhouse that she had no control over us.

*   *   *

I was still on my knees as the interview by the governing Council continued. The questioning went on and on. My studies were discussed and I was asked to explain my understanding of the vows of poverty, chastity and obedience. I answered to the best of my ability and hoped they were satisfied with my explanations.

My age was in question during the interview. The Milwaukee Motherhouse was the American division of the main Motherhouse in Germany. Prior to this, no one as young as eighteen had ever been accepted into the Order in Europe or America. Reverend Mother made an issue of the fact that much would be expected of me.

All the while Reverend Mother was talking to me, I was trying to read the expressions on the other sisters' faces. They didn't look too happy, but they weren't frowning either. Each had a blank expression. Their eyes didn't indicate the outcome either. I had never come in contact with any of them prior to that day. I wished they had been able to really get to know me.

I looked at the five nuns sitting there and thought, "What if it's three to two against me?" I wondered,

"How come five people, who didn't know me, are making such a big decision about my life?" I wasn't feeling very well kneeling there waiting for this to be over.

When Reverend Mother stopped talking, she said the sisters would spend a short time in silence to consider their recommendation. I wasn't wearing a watch, but it felt like forever. After some time, the sisters spoke softly among themselves. I saw heads moving sideways and up and down.

After what seemed an eternity, Reverend Mother addressed each Council member, "Sister, what do you say?"

I held my breath as I listened for the response. I breathed more easily as each sister smiled before replying, "Reverend Mother, I welcome Shirley to our Order." The tension had been so strong that I cried. After Reverend Mother told me to prepare well, all I could say was "Thank you". It didn't take me long to leave the room.

Those next weeks were filled with excitement. We were still having class six days a week and study seven days. We were all measured again for the habits being made for us. That was the only time I remember silence being a problem. We were giddy with excitement for our upcoming investiture into the Novitiate as real nuns.

As postulants, we were told to cleanse our hearts of all worldly attachment. It's funny, when I lived at home, I was always eager to be on the go. I jumped at the chance to go to the movies with my dad when my mother was upset with him. When a new musical came out, I'd convince mother that she wanted to see it and off we'd go. After I entered the convent, those desires just weren't there anymore. I seldom gave thought to what my parents or family were doing. I didn't crave things anymore.

During the weeks following our acceptance into the Order, we observed additional silent periods and put more effort into following the rules laid down for postulants. Our every step was scrutinized.

One exciting task was to submit three names, one of which we hoped to receive when we were presented the habit. Rumor had it that every year someone was given an odd, peculiar or ancient name. I have to admit I wasn't concerned about anybody else's name, I was just hoping I'd be given one of my choices.

One week prior to the installation ceremony of our becoming novices, our group met with two men dressed in business suits and a sister representing the Provincialate. There was one of the five nuns who were in charge of the Order and accepted us for the Novitiate.

The man, who appeared to be in charge, explained that as a member of the Order, any remuneration received for services, material published, or lectures was the sole property of the School Sisters of Notre Dame.

This is something none of us had ever given thought to. We looked at one another in total amazement. Whoever connected going to the convent with money? One girl leaned over toward me and asked, "What about money our folks leave us?" We didn't have long to wait for an answer.

The second man stood and addressed us with a form in his hand saying, "Each of you will be called by name to come up here and sign this form. Besides outside remunerations, any monies left to you as an inheritance will automatically revert to the Order." He told us all forms would need to be signed at this time.

That's just how it happened. We were called by name, walked over to the table, signed the paper, and the two men witnessed our signatures. The legal sized piece of paper had printing on both sides. There was no time allotted to look it over, much less read it, before we signed.

When the two men left, the sister from the Provincialate gingerly tried to convince us that it would only confuse and might upset our parents if we told them about this. When we talked it over during recreation, I found out that the others, as well as I, felt the Provincialate was rather shrewd in the way they handled this. There was no time for us to question a thing. We were all too excited about our approaching big day for any of us to make an issue of this. Good nun that I wanted to be, I never told my parents.

Chapter Eight

On August 4, 1943, at the age of seventeen, I became a novice. "Henceforth," the officiating priest said, "Shirley, you will be known as Sister Mary Marcele." I was given my first choice. This was the day I received the garb of a School Sister of Notre Dame.

We were taken from the nave of the church to a room behind the sanctuary. Everyone could choose someone to help her dress. The sister who befriended me in high school helped me switch from the postulants' long dress to the black habit that had just been blessed during the ceremony.

The habit was beautifully designed. In the front and back were five rows of pleats on each side meeting in the middle. The belt called the cincture held them in place. A small wooden rosary was hung on a hook attached to the cincture. The added fabric of the habit allowed it to flare so gracefully. I could picture myself wearing it as a beautiful gown for dancing.

The headpiece's veil would have been too complicated for me to attach by myself. I felt fortunate to have Sister help me. I remember saying out loud over and over, "I'm a School Sister of Notre Dame. I'm now Sister Marcele."

When everyone was properly dressed, we lined up and again were taken back into the church. It was time for us to profess that we had taken this step freely. As the ceremony continued, we were entrusted with a book called Holy Rule. It spelled out everything we would be expected to do and it explained practices that all sisters of the Order observed. We each promised to study and conduct ourselves according to Holy Rule.

Everything we wore was identical to what the professed nuns wore, except our veil was totally white and theirs was white covered by a black veil. A rosary dangled at our side, but it was nothing compared to the one the professed nuns wore.

Toward the end of the ceremony, a crown of flowers was pinned to the top of our veil. There were beautiful, small, multi-colored, silk buds and blossoms gently woven together interspersed with small green leaves. The crown was reflective of the joy experienced. My strongest memory of that day was the conclusion of the ceremony, when the choir sang "Veni Sponsa Christi," the Latin for "Come, Bride of Christ."

My family and close relatives were invited to attend the lengthy installation ceremony followed by several hours of visitation. I couldn't wait for them to call me by my new name. An elderly aunt came with my parents. My sisters were taking pictures, but occupied most of their time trying to figure out how my veil and headpiece were put on. The time was too short for there to be any serious conversation. It was mostly just chitchat. A bell alerted the visitors that it was time for them to leave.

When my dad hugged me goodbye, he said, "Honey, I'm very proud of you and happy for you."

Our goodbyes were light. By this time it was obvious to my family that I was there to stay.

According to Canon Law, the laws of the Vatican, novices spent one year and one day in total seclusion. We became a close-knit group isolated from other nuns, candidates or postulants. Our wing was separate from the rest of the Motherhouse. We had our own dining room, chapel and sleeping quarters. Our library and classrooms were also separate. In the community room there was a desk for each of us.

Previously, we were not allowed to go anywhere near the novitiate wing. In my mind, this place where I now found myself was sacred ground. And now, I was really here. It took quite a while to sink in that I was actually a novice. I was thrilled to be a member of the Order.

I would say over and over, "I did it. I earned this by myself. My family and relatives never thought I'd amount to anything and here I am."

We had absolutely no communication with our families. No newspapers, letters or gifts. The only thing that remained the same was six days of classes and seven days of study. Besides studying Holy Rule, we had regular college classes. I remember ethics, logic, literature, history and a strong emphasis on methods of teaching.

We were blessed with a wonderful Novice Mistress. Her body might have been slight, but she had a heart full of love and compassion. It was her responsibility to teach us the rigors and disciplines of religious life. She was always there if anyone was ill or needed someone to talk to. The year passed rapidly as we became familiar and accustomed to our new disciplined life.

St. Augustine, who lived in the fifth century, was one of the greatest leaders of the early Christian church. He established a rule of conduct for his monks and members of certain religious Orders. The School Sisters of Notre Dame lived according to this code of life. Our Holy Rule was developed from St. Augustine's teachings and ways.

From the first day in the novitiate, time was devoted each day to the practice of Holy Rule. Some of the first subjects discussed were posture, tone of voice, and the proper gait used in walking, besides all the do's and don'ts of religious life.

The design of the habit provided us with long sleeves that had large openings at the end. We wore tight black wristlets that covered our arms from the wrist past the elbow. Whenever our hands were not engaged in a specific activity, we were to grasp one forearm with one hand and the other forearm with the other hand. This movement brought the two large openings of the sleeves together directly in front of us. Our hands were to be exposed only when we were working with them. The only exception was when we folded our hands in prayer.

As far as walking was concerned, we had already
mastered taking small steps. Now wearing the veil that
was stiffly starched and pinned to the headpiece,
required that we walk at all times as if our head was
being pulled to the ceiling.

During the middle of the first week in our new
surroundings, the Novice Mistress gathered us together
in the community room. It was a Wednesday. Sister
explained that Holy Rule was not intended to make our
life restrictive.

"Community life could become a hornets' nest",
Sister said, "if everyone set their own pattern of
behavior, totally oblivious to the feelings and ways of
others." She added, "The peace you observed in the
Motherhouse these past years was due to uniformity of
conduct and practices."

That made perfect sense to me. We did have peace
and harmony as candidates and postulants. It surprised
me that a group of women of all ages and backgrounds
got along so well.

For some reason that Wednesday, our Novice
Mistress seemed ill at ease compared to the first couple
of days. It was almost as if she were preparing to give
us bad news or bring up something she really didn't
want to talk about.

Sister told us to open our Holy Rule books to a
certain page. One of the novices began to read. This
section of the book described a practice that dated back
hundreds and hundreds of years. All of the religious
orders, for both men and women, which were based on
the rules laid down by St. Augustine, followed a
practice called chapter. Other religious orders followed

similar directives according to the teachings of their founder. Most orders used the term chapter.

The passages explained in great detail the difference between sin, character faults and what I would term sloppy adherence to the practice of Holy Rule.

Sister explained that in no way were we going to be asked to confess our sins publicly, but during a session called chapter, we would voluntarily take turns acknowledging our character faults publicly. These faults would include all infractions of Holy Rule.

These acknowledgments were only to be based on actions that could be observed by another sister, which were infractions of Holy Rule. We didn't have to admit to any wrongful thoughts as we would during formal confession to a priest.

Sister gave us an example. She said each of us would come forward individually and kneel before her and say something similar to the following.

"Sister, I Sister so-and-so, acknowledge that on three occasions I raised my eyes during the great silence. I left a door slam once. I spoke unkindly to a fellow novice on one occasion. I neglected to help another novice when I had the time and ability to do so."

At the conclusion we were to add, "For these and all my faults, I am sorry and beg for a penance." Accepting a penance is an acknowledgement of repentance. Our Novice Mistress would prescribe something for us to do in reparation. For example, for having allowed a door to slam, we might be asked to kneel for 15 minutes near the door that slammed. The penance could be something simple like a prayer or two.

Sister went on to say that if we neglected to admit an infraction, anyone observing us would be required to include our name plus what was observed when it was their time to give chapter.

This made my head buzz like a bees' nest. My mind came up with so many questions. "How often are we going to have to do this?" "What would my family think if they heard this?" "It is hard enough to come up with sins for confession, now we have to figure out our faults." "Is this going to be only during the novitiate?"

It was obvious to me that this would be hard for most of the other novices. Some of them seemed afraid of everything. I viewed some of them as just plain scaredy-cats. I wondered if some of these girls would have thought twice before taking the habit if they had heard of this before hand.

As I caught my breath and simmered down, I realized that if this was the hardest discipline we have to adhere to, it wouldn't be so bad. I had read enough books about the lives of the saints who had harder disciplines to cope with. I decided then and there that if the saints did it, so could I. That seemed to settle any apprehension I had.

Our Novice Mistress said she would prefer volunteers rather than having to call each novice to come forward. I was sitting toward the back of the room at my desk and didn't see a movement of any veil. After a lengthy silence, I thought, *"Oh, what the heck, somebody has to start."* With that I put up my hand.

I have no idea what I said, but I do remember that I was given a penance. I was to say one Hail Mary for the deceased members of the Order.

I remember saying to myself, *"See, that wasn't so bad."*

Slowly, each of the novices raised their hands and went through the routine.

That evening during recreation, our conversation centered on our chapter experience. Some novices told of how traumatized they were when it was their turn. Some even thanked me for getting things started. One novice, who seemed to know pretty much about professed sisters, told us that we would be doing this every week. Without having a clue, most of us concluded this would probably be a monthly session.

The following morning, our Novice Mistress commended us on how well we had accepted this discipline. We weren't too happy to hear her say, "We will follow the same procedure every Wednesday for the rest of the year."

There were other customs designed to help keep us focused during the course of the day. When we encountered another novice in a corridor or when we entered a room with other novices around, we were to say, "Praised be Jesus Christ." And in turn they would respond, "Praised be Jesus Christ." This was to be our practice at all times other than during the great silence. Great silence was observed from night prayer until after breakfast the next day.

Those minutes in between classes, study and group prayer were directed to silent prayer and contemplation of God. Personal satisfaction and comfort was not to be our goal.

One of the outstanding observations of that year
was how well we all got along. We were of different
ages, different backgrounds and interests. Being
separated from everyone else in the Motherhouse
brought us so close together. Plenty of opportunities
arose that could have sparked confrontation. With the
thought of our Wednesday chapter sessions, none of us
wanted to be caught in an infraction of Holy Rule.

We spent time in prayer and meditation, and
chanting our breviary. The breviary contains many of
the hundred fifty Psalms, other parts of the Bible,
prayers, litanies and writings, all of which make up a
collection called the Divine Office.

The Office was arranged for daily recitation
according to the Latin times of the day. In the novitiate
we chanted the breviary three times daily. Early
morning, before morning prayer, we chanted two
sections called Matin and Lauds. At noon, after saying
the Angeles when the bell chimed, we would chant
what was termed the minor hours, Terce, Sext and
None, which is pronounced known. That bell was the
one several of us as candidates were caught ringing at
an odd hour. In the early evening before dinner, we
chanted Vespers and Compline.

Every member of the Order was obliged to recite
the Office daily, unless excused. I loved hearing our
young voices several times a day chanting the various
hours of prayer.

Most days we were able to use the Adoration
Chapel, which was constructed around 1900. Since its
completion, for twenty-four hours a day and 365 days
a year, at least two people were present in adoration
before the altar. As a candidate and postulant we were
able to volunteer an hour of our free time or study time

for holding vigil. Sisters in residence or the novices covered the evening time and early hours of the morning. The hours from 1 a.m. to 3 a.m. were reserved for the novices.

When we were scheduled to have an hour of adoration time, one of us would waken the other in time to arrive in the chapel before 1:00 am. Twenty minutes before the next hour, one of us would quietly slip out and wake one of the next two who would follow us. I looked forward to finding my name on the schedule.

Sometimes an infraction of a rule, like noisily closing a door, speaking unnecessarily during great silence, or not responding immediately when a bell sounded, required that we forego one of our treasured night hours.

The chapel was magnificent. The ceiling, the walls, the floor, and the altar were covered with an exquisite white marble that had soft gray and light blue veins subtly swirling through it. Eight stained glass windows were spaced evenly behind and above the altar. Biblical images were embossed in soft gentle tones on the windows.

There were many candles on the altar surrounding an ornate gold monstrance that held a large host wafer for the worshippers to view. The chapel held enough pews to accommodate several hundred people. Dimly lit sconces provided the only electrical light to guide our steps as we entered and left the chapel. The flickering wicks of the candles cast dancing shadows to keep our eyes focused on the altar.

It's almost impossible to re-create in my mind the peace and awe experienced in those special hours. No

effort was required to lose oneself in quiet
contemplation and prayer. It was as if we were having
a private audience with God Himself.

Chapter Nine

During this year as novices, we were given daily work assignments. The first half of the year I was assigned as an assistant to the sacristan in the Relic Chapel. Novices used the Relic Chapel for meditation, daily Mass, night prayer and for confessions.

It was a great honor for the nun chosen to be the sacristan in any of the chapels. It was her responsibility to prepare the altar for services that were conducted.

Besides dusting and vacuuming the sanctuary, I helped the sacristan change the altar linens, lay out the priest's vestments and on rare occasions, I was allowed to handle the chalices used during a service. In those days, we were not allowed to touch any of the sacred vessels without covered hands.

What made it difficult for me was that the sacristan sister was not connected to the novitiate in any way. This meant I was not allowed to verbally communicate with her. Some days she would give me a note, or at times she spoke to me, but I had to answer with a nod, a facial expression, or my hands. The times I slipped up and spoke, I had to acknowledge at chapter. The sister sacristan was patient with me, but at times I would be distracted concentrating on not talking.

The Relic Chapel was for the private use of the novices. It was like a loft all along the upper side of the big convent church. The ceiling of the church was so high, that from the nave of the church, no one in the church could see into our Chapel.

This chapel housed thousands of canonized Saints' relics. These relics were objects esteemed and venerated because of some association with a saint or martyr. Frequently the relic would be a tiny bone chip or some hair preserved under glass and encased in gold attached to a small pedestal base. The chapel was lined with hundreds of ornate little shelves that held the display.

The second half of the year my responsibility was to take care of our Novice Mistress's office and sitting room adjacent to it. She would entertain other sisters who came to visit with her. I think it was her haven, where she could be away from us for a while. I'd water her plants and see that the rooms were vacuumed and dusted. There was no straightening up that ever had to be done. Sometimes I would remove coffee cups or little plates if one of the other nuns brought her a treat. I felt as if I had the best work assignments of anyone.

Several times a week we had a sewing period. As professed sisters we were going to have to know how to sew the black veil onto a heavily starched white linen strip, seven inches wide and two yards long. Small straight stitches were required for attaching the corded side of the black veil to the starch strip. When worn, the center front of the white strip and veil would be dented down forming a heart shape. The bottom of the heart shape dent would be pinned to a white linen strip that was tied from the forehead to the back of the head. Two more black pins were inserted above the ears through the black veil, the starched attached strip, and the rest of the headgear.

The soft part of the veil hung gracefully over the back. To keep the veil from billowing as we walked, a pleat would be pinned down the back. The width of the pleat was dependent on the size of each sister.

Those sewing days were exciting for us. As we sewed we'd whisper how excited we were to be soon receiving the black veil.

I was very happy with the life I had chosen. The thought of ever wanting to leave never entered my mind. It is obvious from the conversation during our recreation period that the other novices were as happy as I. There was no shortage of smiles, laughter and just plain foolishness. There was a lot of harmless teasing and simple pranks played on each other. It was important for each of us not to take ourselves too seriously. There was no sense pretending we were overly pious.

August 5, 1944 arrived before we knew it. Our novitiate of one year and one day was ending. That morning there was a feeling of excitement and anticipation in the air. We had practiced the installation ceremony and the professing of our vows. As nuns we vowed to live inwardly and outwardly the vows of poverty, chastity and obedience. It was exciting to realize our parents and relatives would join us that day when we officially became real nuns.

The state of Wisconsin was divided into five dioceses. A bishop, appointed by the archbishop of the state, had jurisdiction over the Catholic laity and religious orders for men and women. It was customary that the bishop of the diocese where the motherhouse or monastery was located would preside over the installation of their new members. Because the School Sisters of Notre Dame was a semi-cloistered Papal order, the bishops did not officiate.

Each year a representative from the Archdiocese of Milwaukee was asked to preside over the impressive ceremony. Each novice from the area could submit the name of a dignitary she knew. I suggested our pastor because if he hadn't told my dad to let me go, I wouldn't have been able to reach my goal.

I wasn't too surprised when I heard the day before our ceremony that my pastor, Monsignor Stehling, would preside. Most of the novices were from out of town and my pastor was from the city. After all, he was a Monsignor. I considered it a great honor. Unless Monsignor told my parents ahead of time, I knew they would be so pleased and surprised to see him up at the altar.

The large pipe organ sent out majestic sounds as we walked in pairs down the center aisle of the church. The choir again sang "Veni Sponsa Christi", Come Bride of Christ. Five or six rows of pews had been removed in front. There was a small obscure mark on the floor of the church where each of us was to stand.

Reverend Mother spoke to the congregation about our year in seclusion, praising us for our efforts and dedication. She explained that we were prepared now to be sent on mission. I think she was alerting our families of the possibility that we might be sent to other states, not necessarily near the cities we came from. Her words affirmed that the family umbilical cord had been severed and that our work for God was beginning.

I remember we sang a hymn. We had practiced so much with the music director that our 18 voices filled the church without the benefit of organ accompaniment. I think it was a good release for some of our excitement.

As part of the ceremony, we would change from the white veil to the black veil. Two sisters stood beside each of us as we approached the altar individually. With our backs to the congregation, one sister loosened the white veil. The other sister held the black veil over our head. The white veil was pulled away and the black one set in place and fastened. After the veil was pinned, we walked back to our place in the front of the church. Never before in my life had I ever felt so exhilarated.

We were given our fifteen-decade rosary that would hang at our side fastened to our cincture. I was as honored to carry that rosary as a warrior might wear his armor. Whenever my hand came to rest at my side, it would remind me of my commitment to the Lord and it served as a badge of courage to fulfill any responsibilities given me. At the time of receiving it, little did I know how important a role it would play in years to come.

As a group, we prostrated ourselves face down on the cold marble floor and inwardly surrendered our life to God. A large pall, a black cloth, was laid over us symbolic of our being dead to the world. I remember turning my mind to God and with a heart full of gratitude, thanked God for the privilege of being one of His. I gladly surrendered my mind and heart, looking forward to living and working for God.

We individually professed our vows for a period of three years. After that, with the permission of the Provincial Council, we would be allowed to renew our vows for another three years. After the six years, again with approval, we could profess our vows for life. That meant we could never be dismissed from the Order, no matter what we did or how ill we became. If and when we chose to leave, it could only be arranged through the Vatican in Italy.

At the close of the ceremony a lacquered crown of thorns was placed on our heads and pinned to our veil. This was to remind us that we were beginning our life of penance committed to God. We didn't look at the crown of thorns as something ominous, but rather as a symbol of the dedication we had professed that day.

Quite a few people came to be with me. Besides my parents, sisters, several aunts and cousins, a non-Catholic friend of mine came. She found it hard to comprehend what I was doing with my life. On the whole, this visit was more jubilant than any others had been. The family seemed to be as happy to see me, as I was to see them, after the year of seclusion.

That day was particularly important to me. I had never excelled in anything or succeeded in accomplishing many things before in my life. It felt good to drink in all the praise that I could. It wasn't a point of being proud, but more like a boost to my delicate self-esteem.

After several hours of visiting in the courtyard, it was time to end our day. Prior to my parents' leaving, I sent the crown of thorns home with them as I had done with the crown of flowers the year before.

Closing the door behind them symbolized the beginning of our life of dedication to God. The next week we were busy renewing old acquaintances in the Motherhouse after our year of separation. It was noticeable that recreation periods were longer than usual. On our last Sunday we were given permission to talk during lunch and dinner.

The rumor-mill was in effect. We asked some of the more friendly sisters, "Have you heard where any of us are going to be sent?" I don't think anyone other than those in authority knew the plans, but it was fun speculating where and what grade we'd be teaching.

The day our mission assignments were released, I was packed and ready.

Packing wasn't a big thing. I was given two more habits and two extra veils. Gathering the underclothes, sleepwear and shoes, took a very short time. My parents bought a trunk that I used. It was shipped out to my mission our last week in the Motherhouse. I knew nothing of its destination.

Dad gave me a small overnight case to use the day I left to travel to my mission. I carried my toiletries, which consisted of a comb, brush, toothbrush and small jar of baking soda for brushing. We were each given folders to take anything we composed or created that could possibly be of use later.

Word came that I would be sent to the Fox River Valley area of Wisconsin as a primary teacher.

I felt frightened and apprehensive leaving this secure home and all the friends I had made. We had come to rely on each other very much. We wouldn't be

together again for three years until we came back to
the Motherhouse to renew our vows.

The wonder of what was coming was
overwhelming. Flashbacks of my unpleasant
experience practice teaching haunted me. I told myself
I had grown up and had to move on.

Chapter Ten

Memories of the Motherhouse had disrupted the task of removing my habit for the last time. After placing the 15-decade rosary on the bed, I hesitated. Maybe I could just take this as a remembrance, I thought. I loved the feel of the beads at my side and the little jingling sound it made as I walked. I knew it wasn't mine to keep, so I decided to leave it on the bed.

Regular rosaries have five sets of 10 beads for prayer. There are three different intentions when saying the rosary. The rosary we wore had all 15 sets of 10 beads. Because our rosary was so long, there were several little rings inserted at intervals, which were placed on a hook attached to our belt.

I unclasped the belt I wore around my waist called a cincture. My thoughts went back to the novitiate when it was explained that when girding myself with the cincture, I was fortified with fidelity, constancy and

virginal purity. For the moment, I had a fleeting
thought, Am I betraying my God?

I refused to give credence to any negative thought,
believing it was right for me to leave. I treasured and
respected convent life, Holy Rule, the habit,
community living and working lovingly with children.
I couldn't live the life of a hypocrite. It wasn't enough
observing my vows outwardly. I was required to live
the vow of obedience inwardly as well.

I removed the long wristlets that covered our arms
to the elbow. They were made of black tubing and
hemmed at the ends. My arms looked like alabaster
compared to the top of my hands, which were darker
from many summers' suns.

I unhooked the neckline of the habit. In spite of a
slight hesitation, I removed it, unable to decide how to
lay it on the bed. I kissed it as I had done every day
before putting it on and taking it off. The habit was
blessed and very dear to me. It felt heavy in my hands
as I placed it on the bed making sure the pleats were in
order.

I never dreamed I would be leaving this sanctuary I
called home.

*   *   *

Quickly my thoughts drifted to the first time I wore
the habit outside the Motherhouse. I was one of the last
of the new sisters to leave on mission that day. It was a
time of teary goodbyes for all of us, as one after the
other left. We knew it would be three years until it was
time to renew our vows back at the Motherhouse.

I remember stepping out of the convent entrance on
the day a male volunteer drove me to the train station. I
was so proud to be seen in the beautiful habit. In my

heart I knew I wore it as a shield that protected me from others seeing my fear. Here I was, only eighteen years old and all alone, going to a strange area in the state not knowing what to expect. The Motherhouse had become my haven, my home.

The driver carried my small suitcase and opened the back door of the car for me. I hadn't been in a car for three and a half years. As I glanced around, the streets looked different to me. I had almost forgotten how they looked. Not a word was exchanged between the driver and me. I didn't know what to say and he probably didn't know either. I felt very uncomfortable.

At the train station the driver again carried my case. He handed me my ticket after showing me where to wait. I smiled and thanked him as he walked away. I really wanted him to wait with me. I didn't know what to do.

I had been given one-dollar bill and a dollar in change. My first impulse was to call my dad and tell him where I was. It was time to dismiss that urge. I told myself that I was merely moving from one sacred house to another. Everything would be fine.

Dressed as I was, people walking by looked at me. Some smiled and I didn't know if I should smile back. I had forgotten if it was proper to smile at strangers.

There I stood so prim and proper, like a statue, with my arms in my sleeves. My little case sat silently on the ground next to me. I wished I had someone to talk to or at least something to hold my attention, rather than just standing there not knowing where to look. What a relief when I heard the train coming.

The step was so high to get on the train, I was afraid the habit would get caught on the high step. As I entered the car, I took the first available seat. This was my very first train ride.

As I watched the people enter the car and settle in, I observed so many different facial expressions. A few seemed happy and carefree, others sad. Some were frowning and even seemed depressed. I saw wrinkled brows that carried the look of worry. Some appeared tired after a long trip they had already experienced and probably were heading home.

Having lived those years away from the world, I had forgotten that life was moving forward for those on the outside. From the look on some of the faces, it was apparent things had not been as serene for them as they had been for me. I had something with me to read, but was too interested in the other passengers.

I was bursting to tell them that this was my first train ride, and I was going to the Fox River Valley where I had never been before, and that I was going to be a new primary teacher. I hadn't had the chance prior to this, to tell anyone outside the convent about my new adventure.

When I received my assignment, I was able to send a card to my parents giving them the new address where I would be. Calculating mail delivery time, I assumed they would have gotten the news the day I was on the train. I made a point of telling them that on the second Sunday of every month, I would be able to have visitors two to three hours in the afternoon. I wondered if they would be willing to make the two-hour ride.

The sounds of the world around me were intriguing. It had been some time since I heard a man's voice loudly lamenting some situation. From the front of the train car, I could hear a baby crying. A couple of kids ran up and down the aisle.

I remember thinking to myself, *I'm back in the world again.*

Chapter Eleven

As I stepped off the train, a woman with a kind smile came over to me, introduced herself, and said she was a parishioner of the church school where I would be teaching. She carried my little suitcase to and from the car as the man had done. I thought I should be the one carrying the case because both drivers were my elders. Suddenly I realized wearing the habit drew respect. I was glad they didn't know there was a frightened young girl inside that habit.

We exchanged pleasantries on the ride and the driver pointed out a few landmarks. She showed me the post office, a pet store, and a drug store. When passing a new building, she said their city was one of the first to have a day-care center for children while their parents worked. She seemed proud to tell me her daughter worked there.

The woman parked the car in the driveway outside the convent next to the school. When we reached the back door, she rang the bell and turned to leave. I barely had enough time to say thank you.

A tall, rather pretty sister opened the door with a smile and told me to come in. After telling her I was assigned there, she welcomed me and asked me to follow her into the community room. It was an extraordinarily big room with lots of windows on three sides. I could see the school, church and playground from two sides and across the street, homes with children playing.

There were 24 large desks set in units of four in the room. Close to the entry door was a roll top desk. As I entered the room, a stately sister rose from behind the oversized roll top desk and smiled a welcome as she walked toward me.

I had practiced in my mind so many times the way I was to greet my new superior. Her demeanor made it very easy for me to just say, "Sister Superior, I'm Sister Marcele from the Motherhouse."

Her welcome was so joyful and sincere; I knew I was blessed with a perfect mission.

After the exchange of a few words, she asked a sister to show me to my cell. We went to the second floor and then up another flight of stairs to the attic. At first I was apprehensive when I thought I was going to be sleeping in an attic. The steps weren't carpeted or even covered. As I stepped into the attic, I saw a neat arrangement of trunks on the left. On the right were groups of storage boxes. It was then my eyes looked upward and I saw many electrical wires extending the full length of the attic. They were just hanging there precariously.

At the far end of the attic I saw two doors. One opened to a powder room and the other to a bedroom with twin beds and two dressers. I found I would be sharing a room with one of the high school teachers. I thought the convent house looked too big for just a grade school. Now I knew why there were so many desks in the community room.

Sister helped me put my few things away and informed me they'd been notified that my trunk would arrive the following day. Sister told me to hurry because Sister Superior had said she would grant some recreation time when we got back downstairs.

As we reentered the community room, one by one the sisters introduced themselves and welcomed me. I was amazed at the extreme age difference. Some sisters looked rather old to me. I guess when you're 18, anyone in their 60s and over looks old.

Some sisters asked me where I came from, and how I heard of our Order. They joked about my looking so young. I wasn't about to tell them how young I really was. Dressed as they, I only had to see that I acted maturely.

It felt funny speaking so casually to nuns. They seemed so down to earth. I remembered how awkward it felt when I was a student in high school, when a sister pulled me aside to tell me something or ask a question. Here I was, going to be working as one with them.

The next stop was in the kitchen where I met the house sisters, a cook, and laundress. Larger missions like ours were fortunate to have extra help.

Before long, a bell rang and I was informed it was time to say the afternoon breviary. I followed the others to the chapel. It was a quaint small room with an old fashioned altar. The altar was white with gold paint trimming. The backdrop had two tiers with candles on one level and a few holy pictures on another. The front of the altar itself had a raised image of the Christ child. There were small church pews on the left and the right of the chapel itself.

I could see the room couldn't hold any more than 30 people comfortably. It was apparent that this house was previously a big family home. The chapel probably was a small bedroom. The closet on the side held candles, altar cloths and so on.

We said the hours of Vespers and Compline together out loud followed by 30 minutes of quiet meditation. Sitting there I felt at home. I knew I was the youngest kid on the block, but I wasn't being made to feel that way. Everyone seemed so friendly. From my experience of practice teaching I had drawn pictures in my mind of everyone finding fault with me.

The bell rang for dinner. We left the Chapel quietly and went into the refectory. Three long tables were set crosswise in the room. I was seated at the last place at the last table. The seating was arranged according to the years one was professed. Over the years to come, I was able to move up a couple of chairs. Every group of four settings was served family style by the cook and laundress. Each week a different person did the spiritual reading during the meal.

The cook was a German woman, so she prepared food similar to what I was used to at home. We never wanted for food, but there was one thing difficult for me to accept. If cookies were the dessert, there would be four little cookies on a plate, one for each of us.

Puddings and ice cream were served in very small dishes too. My sweet tooth was begging for extras.

The four sisters most recently professed cleared the tables. The best part of all was that we were never asked to do the dishes.

Recreation followed immediately after dinner. Recreation was free time, but it had to be spent in the community room. In addition to all the desks, there was a long table placed somewhat near a row of bookcases with glass doors located near the entry door. A sister told me that if we ever needed more room to work on a project, the table would be a great help.

During recreation the table was a busy spot for games or cards. Canasta was hot in those days. I saw some sisters playing Chinese checkers. A small nucleus of sisters worked on their knitting or embroidery while they chatted. The hour seemed to be over quickly. During the day we were only allowed to go to our cell with permission. Except when at prayer, meals, or at school, all our time was to be spent in the community room.

When recreation was over, those who chose went to early night prayer at 7:00 p.m., after which they were expected to retire. Second night prayer was at 9:30 p.m. with lights out for everyone at 10 p.m.

Those of us who chose later night prayer, gathered in the community room. I was shown the desk I would occupy while I lived there. Sitting at the desk, I could see an alcove to the right of the Superior's desk. I went to check it out. I saw a mimeograph machine, two typewriters, paper of all sizes and color, and a great deal of art supplies. It looked like a fun spot.

As time wore on, the sister who sat opposite me turned out to be a very good friend of mine. She was an excellent teacher eager to share her expertise. Currently she was a sixth grade teacher who started out with a primary class also. Sister heard I would be teaching third grade. That evening she gathered up some textbooks for me to look at during the quiet time before second night prayer.

I was so excited about seeing my classroom; I found it hard to wait until the next day.

To alert us to chapel at 9:30 p.m., a sister rang a small table bell so as not to awaken those who had retired. Early morning and during the day, a loud sounding bell summoned us for various activities.

I again took my place in the chapel. I found that we said the identical night prayer on mission that we used in the Motherhouse. It amazed me to see that so much of our life in the Motherhouse was adapted to mission life.

Following night prayer, the Great Silence began. This meant from night prayer until after breakfast the following morning we observed total silence. We learned in the Motherhouse that total silence did not mean just vocal sounds. The Great Silence meant whether we were handling objects, walking down a corridor, opening or closing doors, or taking off our shoes while preparing for bed, everything was done without a sound. To help us maintain inner as well as outer silence, the Great Silence also meant not catching the eye of another person. Great Silence was observed on mission, just as we had in the Motherhouse.

After prayer, I found my way back up to the attic. The stairway was barely lit from a dim bulb hanging in the middle of the attic ceiling. Everything was eerie. On top of that, I was frightened as I stood at the top of the stairs.

Suddenly in the gloomy darkness I didn't know what was happening. I felt something flying all around me, making a swishing sound. I could tell there was more than one thing swooping past me. That night I learned bats do not fly in the daytime, but they do at night. Thank goodness we never found one in the bedroom.

My roommate told me later she had meant to warn me about the bats at evening recreation, but decided I could find out for myself. The only suggestion she gave was, "Keep your head down and walk fast."

It didn't take me long to get used to the little creatures.

I found out that going upstairs during an electrical storm brought its own form of excitement. There were a lot of wires strung this way and that way throughout the attic. In the midst of thunder and lightning, sparks would flash from all directions from these wires. It was a wonder nothing ever caught fire. There was no possible escape route if something had happened. I would have been pleased to sleep on a bench in the Chapel rather than up there during a storm.

All things considered, over the next few weeks, I was pleased to find out we had the nicest bedroom of all, in spite of our fluttering friends and potential fireworks. I felt special, because there were only two of us using the powder room upstairs. Others in the house were not that fortunate.

I couldn't have had a better roommate. Sister taught the high school seniors history and literature. She had quite a reputation among the students. I found out something that apparently became a ritual with her. At the beginning of every class on the first day of school, Sister would ask the boy who had a reputation for being most mischievous or troublesome, to open a designated classroom window. After several futile attempts by the boy to open the window, Sister would walk over and push that window up as if it were as simple as could be. She would turn to the class and say, "If there's any trouble with anyone in this class, they'll have to answer to me." Knowing the janitor always had trouble with that window, Sister knew that was a good way to get their attention.

When Sister was growing up, her father sold fresh fruit and vegetables at an open market in downtown Milwaukee to grocers and restaurant owners. Sister was tall, slim, and very strong from working with her dad. She told us how she could carry at the same time two long bunches of bananas, holding a stem in each hand.

As the year progressed, I found the students loved Sister as much as the rest of us did. She was a great teacher, a friend to all, and everyone knew she meant business.

One strange thing about my roommate was that in spite of the fact that our heads were covered at all times, she wanted to have her hair trimmed in a specific way. She had a beautiful dark head of hair. After we got to know each other better, Sister explained that no one was able to cut her hair the way she wanted it. Somehow she trusted me. Over time, and after a great deal of directions and practice, I was able to cut her hair just the way she wanted it. In turn, she always cut mine.

After a night's good sleep, morning prayers and breakfast, the other third grade teacher took me over to the school to see my classroom. What a thrill stepping into the room and thinking to myself, *this is all mine*. In two weeks and a couple of days, my own little children would be sitting there.

Two walls were covered with blackboard; a third had a large bulletin board and a doorway leading to the cloakroom. The remaining wall had very large windows. I counted 42 little desks. Sister told me I would probably start out with 39 or 40 students, but a few more might come as the year progressed.

Reality hit me as sister turned to leave the room and said, "You have the next couple weeks to decorate the bulletin board over the blackboards and the large board in the back of the room. In the closet behind you, you'll probably find some leftover things from the previous teacher. In the supply room you'll find the textbooks needed for the children. While there, pick up a lesson plan book, and see that you have the first week's work outlined for Sister Superior to inspect before school starts."

With that, she was gone. I wanted to be afraid, but decided I had too much to do to let myself be overwhelmed.

Time sped by. I found construction paper, crayons, India ink, scissors and pins to get me started. I came across a cut out of Snow White and the dwarfs. The bulletin board was large enough to create a pathway of paper stones. I lettered each stone with the name of one of our class subjects on them. With trees in the background, I tried to make it look as if Snow White and her friends were walking down the path of learning. The decorated room looked beautiful to me. It took me more than a week to get things ready.

A seating chart lay on my desk and name cards were on top of each of the children's desk.

Chapter Twelve

The first day of school arrived. Prior to that day, Sister Superior worked with me sometime during the day and every evening, answering many questions and helping me prepare my first week's lesson plan. I ate up every word she said.

It didn't take me long to realize that I had been blessed with a wonderful mentor. I found out that throughout the Order, Sister Superior was considered an outstanding teacher of children and teacher of teachers. Every weeknight the first year, I sat beside her as we went over every class period and subject for the following day.

Sister Superior dropped into our classroom every day. At times she asked if she could watch what the children were doing, while I would be presenting some material. She had a way of putting me at ease so I looked forward to her being there.

Sometimes she'd come in, wink at me and say, "Sister, I miss teaching little children so much. Would you mind if I taught for a while?"

Of course I'd invite her to take over and I took notes of how she did things. I learned so much from her. I was given help and guidance most new teachers never receive. Sister's love for the wondrousness of children rubbed off on me.

As the year went on, I remember vividly thinking to myself that I was always sorry when Friday came around. I couldn't wait for Monday morning to come. On the weekend I felt separated from my little family. The three years this great woman was my superior went by so quickly.

Those years brought quite a variety of teaching. The first year I taught third grade. The second year I taught second and third grade. The third year second grade.

That third year proved to be very different. I had a larger classroom and 47 second graders. A newly professed sister was assigned 35 second graders. Before the end of the first month of school, she had severe emotional problems. She cried frequently during class and became severely depressed.

One Friday after the children were dismissed, Sister Superior explained I would have an additional 25 children in my class. Before I knew it, the janitor and his helper were bringing in desk upon desk to my room. There would be 10 students in the other second-grade and 72 in mine. The prospect of an overflowing classroom frightened me, but considering the circumstances, it had to be done.

I know this sounds overwhelming, but it turned out to be one of the most memorable years of my teaching experience. Being young, I had a lot of energy and enthusiasm. Discipline was never a problem for me in the classroom. No, I didn't use a ruler. The children learned that certain look I gave them. That's all that was needed.

In the 1940's, phonics was the preferred method of teaching reading. We played games around the phonics principles. The children loved it. Each of the 72 children read aloud to me at least once every three days. While I drilled the addition and subtraction facts with half the class, the other half, working in pairs, were reciting the sums and remainders to each other. Our days were planned, and we stuck to the plan.

I learned to be so organized and on top of every situation. I would plan each project ahead of time in my mind. Sister Superior was invited one day to drop in and observe 72 pair of hands finger painting at the same time. I know she could tell the children and I enjoyed every minute of it. To my amazement, no paint spilled on the floor and not a pail of water was overturned when they washed their hands. We let the papers dry overnight on their desks and the next morning we had fun decorating the room with them.

When we studied poetry, I encouraged everyone to write several poems. The class decided they wanted to make a book of their poems. Using a uniform piece of paper, each child was able to select the favorite poem they composed. It took several weeks to compile the neatest paper they could write, because only their best could go into this book. They designed the cover and learned what it was like to make a table of contents. The father of one of the children worked for a book binding company. The bound book of 72 poems was a big hit when we had open house.

Sister Superior's responsibilities extended beyond just our Order. She was requested to sponsor teaching demonstrations to help our teachers and those from various Orders improve their teaching skills. Nuns came from many surrounding cities to participate on designated Saturdays.

Sister prepared me to be the presenter for subjects pertaining to the primary grades. I loved being on stage - that was the ham in me coming out.

The biggest challenge I had was to try to anticipate how the children would respond.

Occasionally I had to delicately stop a fight or gently discourage a child from unacceptable behavior. At times the children decided to be shy and not responsive. I'd have to quickly dream up something to put them at ease so they would participate.

Choral speaking was in at that time. It is the recitation of poetry or prose in unison. The children are required to memorize the material and then recite it so specifically and attentively that it sounds as if only one voice is heard.

I prepared a program of recitations for all of the second and third grade students. The teachers saw to it that the children memorized the poems. Many times I practiced with the entire group during school time and sometimes after school. The program was presented for the parents and student body an hour before the children were dismissed on a Friday. Parents always love seeing their little ones on display. Grandparents and parents were surprised the youngsters could undertake such a disciplined project.

In those days the second graders made their first Communion during the month of May. For four years it was my responsibility to prepare the youngsters for their big day. Besides the 80 to 90 children in our second grades, there were always 15 to 20 others from the public school joining us. They were given religious instruction and Communion preparation at our school on Saturdays. I took the responsibility of preparing them and our second graders very seriously, because I wanted their day to be as special as my teacher had made it for me years ago.

About a month before their Communion day, these same little ones made their first confession. It was so hard to talk to them about sin because they were so sweet and innocent. I remember well not allowing myself to smile when they wanted to practice for me what they were going to say in the confessional.

They came up with statements like, "I punched my brother six times."

Another said, "I told my mother that my brother took the candy, but I did."

It was easy to tell they were nervous because of the pained look on their little faces. When I took them over to church for this first experience, each one wanted to be last in line.

The biggest challenge on their first Communion day, was to get the hundred and some pair of feet to walk two by two down the long aisle of the church. As much as they wiggled and as poorly as they did at practice, they always surprised me on the day itself.

I could come up with no other explanation than that a special angel must have hovered over each of them. They looked like little angels, the girls dressed in their pretty white dresses and veils. I hardly recognized the boys so neat and trim and clean in their white shirts and ties and wearing their dark long trousers. I was always so proud of them.

Each summer most of the teachers at our mission went off for various summer school programs, to take a full load of classes. I went to a college about 45 miles away. We shared morning and night prayer with sisters of our Order, but were on our own saying our breviary. It felt like a vacation because we were with lay people and members of other Orders who didn't observe daytime silence as we did.

The third summer after returning from school, I spent ten days at the Motherhouse to renew my vows for another three years. It was fun to see all the sisters with whom I spent my novitiate year.

On the second day there, we were called one- by-one to present ourselves before the leaders of the Order to beg permission to renew our vows. Our number went from 18 to 17 that day. Gossip had it, that the reason one of our group was refused permission to stay in the Order was that she had become too friendly with the pastor at her mission. We never got to say goodbye to her; she was just gone.

On our third day we began a silent seven-day retreat as we had before taking our first vows. It was wonderful to drink in the atmosphere of the Motherhouse again. Our tenth day was filled with excitement and goodbyes. We looked forward to gathering together again in three years to profess our final vows.

Returning to the Fox Valley, I found that four of our sisters were being transferred to other schools. The hardest thing for all of us was to learn our beloved Sister Superior was leaving. Sister was elected by the membership of the Order to the highest office. She went to Milwaukee as Reverend Mother, the head of the whole Order. I missed her so. I never realized how attached I had grown to her until she was gone. Sister was so humble. I knew she was not eager to leave because she never sought glory for herself.

When the new assignments were announced, everything moved quickly. Two days later our sisters left and the new replacements arrived. I felt compassion for some who had been at the house for ten years. They had to pick up and leave in two days. I imagined it would be traumatic. We had been taught never to be attached to anyone or anything. I marveled at the way the whole procedure just flowed.

There was much speculation as to who would be our new Sister Superior. When she arrived we saw quite a contrast in appearance between her and our former Superior.

The new Superior was not tall and stately like the previous one. Sister was more animated and demonstrative. Her swift movements made it look as if she were floating. We soon learned that even though Superior had a different way of governing us, she had a beautiful heart.

The fourth, fifth and sixth year I was reappointed to the second-grade, but was left very much alone as to what I did in my classroom and how I did it. The new Sister Superior had a phrase she liked to repeat when we asked questions. "You know your responsibility. Do it."

Though Sister was the principal of our grade school, checking up on us was not a priority with her. Sister had been a high school teacher for years and maybe didn't know how to relate to little children. I fared very well under her charge, but wondered what it would have been like for me if I hadn't had the earlier guidance from the former Superior.

This Sister Superior enjoyed our recreation periods so much that she didn't have a hard time finding occasions to celebrate. On Saturdays or Sundays she would designate a couple of hours in the afternoon as extra recreation time besides our one hour after dinner. Some sisters just enjoyed sitting around talking, while others were quick to set up a game or find a deck of cards. I had been a game and card player all my life. I taught the sisters card games they had never heard of before. Canasta and Casina turned out to be their favorites.

The same year the new Sister Superior arrived, a new music teacher came to take over the high school chorus and serve as one of the organists for the church. The sister who previously handled these tasks was a grade school teacher, but as an accomplished pianist, she filled the role well.

This new music teacher was quite a character. Many of the other sisters in the house thought her odd and peculiar. Her fellow sisters were never mean to her, but ignored her because she was different.

I think her idiosyncrasies were due to her many talents. Everything she said and did would spring from her with a dramatic flare. The sound of her voice made it seem as if she'd break out in song any minute. As she spoke, her words were emphasized by her hands like someone conducting an orchestra. She was fun to be with; I really enjoyed her.

Sister often came to me and asked for help. Many times she didn't know where to go when the bell rang. It seems she was always misplacing something or other. Often during recreation Sister played old songs and I sang with her. Before long she asked if I'd direct the chorus because she wanted to do the accompaniment. Sister Superior thought it a great idea.

I was under the impression that my involvement was only for practices, but learned it meant performances also. Parents flocked to several concerts during the year. Regional competitions were held in Green Bay, Wisconsin. The high school chorus competed every year.

It was a rule of our Order that, whenever we were outside the convent, another sister had to accompany us. Because I helped Sister, I was the logical one to go with her. Several of the children's parents rode with the students on the bus. A parish volunteer drove Sister and me.

These were fun excursions. I felt like a mother hen keeping my eye on Sister, even though she was about 30 years older than I. Many a time, I had to remind her that we were not to go into fabric shops, which she longed to visit. She'd ask me to find a store with an elevator just because she liked elevators. When walking to our destination, if we went past a pet store, Sister would have to stop and say hello to every animal in the window and give them a name.

I often had my hands full, not because of the children or the parents that were along, but because of this eccentric musical genius. And genius she was. Not only did she compose beautiful music, but she had a talent for bringing out the best in young voices. The complicated music she taught the high school students out shown others in competition. With her at the helm, our high school always won the competitions.

Chapter Thirteen

Shortly after the new music sister arrived, our pastor decided he wanted the daily seven o'clock mass to be a High Mass. At that type of mass, parts of the ceremony are sung along with the priest. Sister agreed that she would play the organ and I'd sing. It wasn't unusual that I heard about decisions after they were made. Our morning schedule changed a bit. We didn't join the other sisters for breakfast at 7:00 am. We left morning meditation earlier than the others to attend High Mass.

After the service, we'd hurry back to the convent for a quick breakfast before going to school. I loved it, particularly because I was doing something different than everybody else.

Our Holy Rule prescribed that no sister was to leave the premises without being accompanied by another sister. It worked to my advantage on one occasion.

The second year the music teacher was with us, she decided she needed to have more voice training. After discussing voice lessons with our Superior, she received permission. The music sister then asked if I might be the one to accompany her. It turned out Sister Superior arranged for both of us to have singing lessons at Lawrence College in Appleton. Their conservatory of music was not too far away.

Sister and I were thrilled to go for private voice lessons every Saturday morning for two semesters. It was great fun; we hopped a bus to and from the Conservatory.

I never dreamed I would have an opportunity like this. I couldn't wait to tell my parents. Before their next visit, the music Sister practiced with me to prepare something I might sing for them.

My parents, sister and brother-in-law politely sat through my little performance. I really don't think they were very impressed. The music was semi classical and in Italian. They had only heard me sing popular songs at home. After singing I heard a few forced, "That was nice."

My brother-in-law, not the one who was a soloist, wrinkled his nose and said, "Where did you ever find a voice like that?" I didn't ask what he meant, I was afraid he might tell me.

After Sister left the room, the family conversation centered on the music Sister. The group concluded she was very odd and peculiar. They couldn't get over her dramatically swinging her hands up in the air as she played the piano. I had come to love Sister's unusual ways, it didn't matter to me what my family thought.

Every year the senior class of the high school put on a drama or musical for the parents and school. The head of the English department and the music teacher were responsible for the production.

During the rehearsal weeks, I was relieved of playground duty at lunchtime. In those days, there were no microphones available for the performers. It was my assignment to help the cast project their voice to the back of the room without having to shout.

Every day a different group was selected from a part of a scene to run through their lines for me. We started the sessions when they were still using scripts. I stood in the back of the auditorium and had them repeat their lines until they could be heard well.

Before rehearsals were over, everyone could be heard when they spoke. If they sang, we practiced until every word could be understood also. The students were fascinated to learn that words often were pronounced differently when sung if they were to be clear for everyone in the audience to hear.

Some of the students weren't too happy having to keep repeating lines over and over. After the performances they were proud of themselves when their parents and peers kept saying, "I could hear every word from where I was sitting."

The cast heard the word projection so much, that when the actors saw me around school, they would often say, "Hi, Sister Projection." That name stuck with me year after year.

The third year under the second Superior, I was assigned to teach sixth grade. I was surprised to read over the roster for the year and find some of these children had been in my second or third grade classes.

It turned out to be a year of fun and learning. Most of the children knew me and I knew them. They were familiar with my way of teaching and I was able to recall enough about them that they couldn't bluff me.

The children were experiencing so many changes in themselves at this time. Because of the strong bond we shared, both boys and girls felt free to talk over challenges they were experiencing. The boys were becoming aware of the girls and the girls had their eyes on several of the boys.

Sometimes the youngsters felt they didn't know how to talk to their parents about things on their mind. They just needed someone to listen. It was my place to let them know their parents were young themselves at one time and did have answers for them. I sure didn't have the answers.

The boys in my class thought it shameful that I didn't know how to play chess. They were determined that I should learn. Before class we would start a game, set the board on the filing cabinet during class time and after school finish the game. I stipulated in the beginning that no way were they to allow me to win. I'm not proud to say it took a long time before I won a game. Once I started to win, I think they were sorry they taught me.

That summer I attended St. Norbert College in De Pere. I had planned to take nine credits as usual. Sister Superior told me that St. Norbert's had earlier sent a request for someone to teach Gregorian chant during the summer.

Without mentioning it to me, Sister sent them the name of the chant classes I had taken in the Motherhouse. I wasn't aware she even knew about that or my grades. Sometime later Sister received a request from the College asking if I were available to teach a class that summer. It was decided I would take six credits and teach the class.

It was not unusual for decisions of this kind to be made without consulting me. I had taken a vow of obedience. That meant I was to do whatever my superiors deemed best for me. Actually I was thrilled, but also afraid to be teaching nuns.

I reviewed what I had learned. I had been using the chant when singing the early morning Mass, but never taught it. There were to be six two-hour classes that summer. I had to work very hard to outline the sessions and gradually fill them in with more detail. I made handouts to copy later.

The music sister helped me choose simple selections to be taught in the beginning. I wanted a more substantial selection at the end of the series to emphasize to the sisters how far they would be able to take their students.

Sisters from other Orders would be in my class, veteran teachers themselves I assumed. Sister Superior told me to have confidence and assured me I was prepared. She told me to trust God. She and I both knew that I'd probably be the youngest one there.

The summer session went well. I was blessed with 38 kind teachers who had a good ear for music. They made me feel comfortable. It was my impression they had pity on me because I told them I had never taught this before.

My prep work and handouts helped a great deal. Interest and enthusiasm mounted with each succeeding class. Word around the campus was that others were wondering where the beautiful music came from. They were used to hearing the seminarians at St. Norbert's chanting their breviary, but couldn't figure out why they were hearing women's voices. We took that as a compliment.

When I returned to my mission, I learned that a notice came from the Green Bay diocese stating Gregorian chant was now included in the curriculum of the sixth, seventh and eighth grades in all the Catholic schools.

Gregorian chant was becoming popular in the Catholic Church. Prior to this the chant was sung in the monasteries, but not taught to children. The music is sung from a four line staff with notes formed differently than modern music. I was excited to know that I would be teaching it to my sixth grade class the following year.

Shortly after this, I left to spend a week at the Motherhouse in Milwaukee. I had gone back after the first three years on mission to renew my vows, but now after six years, it was time for final vows.

The first day at the Motherhouse was fun getting acquainted again. It was a good thing we were secluded from others. We had our own wing for that week. There was so much catching up to do. It didn't take long to revive the nicknames we had for each other in the novitiate.

Except for prayer time and mealtime, I don't remember observing any silence during the day. The sister in charge of our preparation for vows made us feel at home. She joined in whatever we were doing.

The next three days we participated in a wonderful silent retreat. The retreat master gave inspirational talks and offered private consultations for those who wanted them.

The day after the retreat ended, we waited for our name to be called. It was time to appear before the Provincialate again to beg permission to be admitted to final vows.

I know I wasn't the only one wondering how many of us would be left in our group this time. It turned out that all 17 of us were accepted. Because parents, relatives and friends were invited to the final vows ceremony, we were all excited to see everyone again.

The day following our acceptance we practiced the renewal ceremony in church. Practicing took a lot of time, but we found plenty of time for fun and teasing one another.

The big relief about taking final vows was that we could not be sent home regardless of what we ever did or how ill we would ever become.

My parents and most lay Catholics thought that final vows meant we could never leave the Order. The commitment on the part of the Order was that we would be taken care of for the rest of our lives.

The afternoon before our renewal ceremony, we assembled in a room and learned we had to add our signature again to the papers we signed before going to the novitiate. This time we would sign as a professed sister.

After we assembled, two laymen and one of the main Sisters of the Order entered the room. They explained that we were to sign the original forms stating any monies or items willed to us as professed sisters would automatically become the sole possession of the Order.

The men were lawyers who were to witness our signatures. Some of the older sisters in our group asked questions. I didn't expect to inherit anything great, so none of this bothered me.

When it was my turn, I went up to the table and signed the paper. There was no question in my mind because everything I needed was provided for me. It seemed only right that anything I received should go to the Order.

On the day of our renewal, the ceremony was long, but very simple. We participated in a Mass and before its conclusion we each recited our vows individually. After the recitation of our vows, we prostrated ourselves on the floor and a black pall was again placed over us as a symbol of surrender and humility while the choir sang a hymn.

My parents and family were present. We gathered in the courtyard after the ceremony and enjoyed some light refreshments. The only vivid recollection I have of that gathering is that my Dad pulled me aside and said, "Are you sure you're happy and that this is what you want?"

I said, "Daddy, I am happy and thanks for letting me go."

I explained to my parents that I was leaving by train the next day to go back to the Fox River Valley. My Dad insisted that it would be very easy for him to drive me there. It would have been wonderful to spend some time alone with him. I could tell he missed me very much.

Unfortunately, the sister in charge of our renewal told us ahead of time that regardless of where our next destination would be, no family member could escort

us. The vow of obedience precluded our ever
questioning. I personally thought this arrangement was
determined in order not to tempt us to stop at our
parents' home.

The following day we gathered our few possessions
and left one-by-one to return to our missions. Some of
the sisters went to new locations, but I returned to my
first place of assignment.

The train ride from Milwaukee was so different
from the first time I left the Motherhouse. I was used
to intermingling with lay people by this time. After all,
I was the ripe old age of 25. I felt so grown up and
mature now, even though it had only been six years
since I left the Motherhouse.

The day after I returned, news came that two
teachers, as well as our Sister Superior, had been
transferred. It was hard enough to have two sisters
leave, but to have another change of superior was
difficult for me. It was apparent that the style, the
manner, the disposition of the superior was pivotal to
the way things flowed in the convent house.

After a teary goodbye to the others, we welcomed
the replacement sisters and awaited our new Sister
Superior.

Chapter Fourteen

One of the sisters recognized a church volunteer's car pulling into the parking lot next to our convent house. We concluded our new Sister Superior had arrived. The sisters who reached the window first watched her get out of the car.

The whispered word around the room was, "She's here - tall, thin and pretty." This time it was the front doorbell that rang and not the back. When the replacement sisters arrived, they entered as I had, from the back door. The practice of humility required that we always use the back entrance. The front door was to admit guests only.

Our meeting this new Sister Superior felt strained. We all rose as she came to the door of the community room. Before saying a word, standing in the doorway, her eyes swept from left to right, observing the room as well as each of us. Her manner told us that we and the house were not what she expected.

Curtly, she said her name and added, "I am the Superior of this house. Get back to work, each of you!"

It wasn't recreation time, so we all sat down and got back to what we were doing. No one said a word or even whispered to one another. I watched the expressions of the sisters around me and read that they were as bewildered as I.

One thing I noticed as Sister Superior stood in the doorway was her posture, because she stood so erect and still. It appeared as if she were incapable of bending or even turning her head. Where were the kind smiles, jovial remarks or even friendly gestures we had loved in the previous Superiors?

Someone showed her to her cell. We didn't see her again until the bell rang for chapel.

The first night at dinner, Sister Superior stopped the sister who was doing the spiritual reading and said, "From now on, see that you are prepared to read. I will not tolerate any mumbling and faltering."

I was so grateful I wasn't the one reading that day.

The following morning began the weekend. Sister Superior called a meeting in the community room. I remember her saying, "When you leave this room there will never ever be anything on your desks."

She stated that earlier she had looked into the room and two of the sisters were not at their desks. She reminded us that, at all times during the day, we were expected to be at our desks unless she had directed us to complete some other task. We knew the rule. It was customary to beg permission to go to our cell if we had forgotten something, but other than that, except for meals or prayer time, we were to be in the community room. Previously, no one ever checked up on us.

On weekends we never went over to school unless some other sister was also working in her classroom. We weren't allowed just to spend a day there. It was fine if we had to pick up something or work on a bulletin board.

Sister Superior indicated the precise place on her desk where we were to leave a note, stating the time we went over to school and with whom. Our previous Superiors knew if we went to school it was for a good reason and we'd be back as soon as we had finished what we had to do. They trusted us to use good judgment.

By the second or third day, it was apparent things were going to be different from now on. The whole atmosphere of the house changed. I noticed that even when walking in a corridor, the sisters didn't look up at each other and smile. Recreation periods were subdued. The fun and laughter wasn't there as it had been before. It was a good thing school was starting in a couple of days.

Sister Superior was an enigma. It was difficult to read her mood because she didn't frown nor did she smile. Sister's expression never changed as she spoke. Even in between her words, she pinched her lips together. Her beautiful complexion was reminiscent of a porcelain doll. We all had an opinion as to how old she was. We knew this was her first assignment as Superior. We decided she was in her mid-to-late 40s.

It was very difficult during recreation time to draw Sister Superior into a conversation. Several of us got together to set up a contest to see which of us could get her to converse the longest. Because the cook sister was one of us, the prize would be an extra dessert. The rule was that we had to have another one of us present to record the time we could keep Sister talking.

The only reason we did this, I think, was that we wanted to create some fun. I wonder what Sister Superior's reaction would have been if she knew we were doing this?

When it was my turn, I started by asking, "What do you like to do during recreation?" I'd have agreed with anything she liked, just to get her to talk. All she did was shrug her shoulders.

I followed with silly questions like, "Did you notice how warm the sun was today?" and "Do you enjoy playing games?" I could barely get her to respond with a yes, no or even a nod.

I can best describe our general observations of Sister by saying it was apparent to everyone who lived in the house, that our Sister Superior's expertise was the art of criticism. Several times a day we would hear that whoever raised the window shades in the community room left one higher or lower than another. Someone thoughtlessly left the bathroom light on. Some sister had the back of her veil pinned too high, and of course, another had hers pinned too low. One sister had to practice bringing her chair out from under her desk and then replacing it again and again to see how quietly she could do it. The corrections went on and on.

What amazed us the most was that before Sister was with us less than a month, she had convinced the Pastor and the church trustees that we needed a new convent house. Two weeks later, ground was broken next door to the current house. Before winter prevented outside work, the structure was set for the workmen to finish the inside.

When out of earshot, we would mimic Sister's favorite words: "This place is appalling, simply appalling." We assumed the only reason action was taken so quickly on the project was that she probably put the fear of God into everyone involved.

The new convent house was a two-story brick building. It provided a private cell for all 24 sisters, a chapel, a refectory and a large community room. Each cell had a bed, a straight chair, a sink (no mirror) a small closet and a chest of drawers. In the beginning of February we moved in.

The old adage rang true, "A house does not make a home."

Most of us enjoyed school starting in September, but we were more eager than ever this year. The only reason the weekends became bearable were because the weekdays brought some relief. I was eager to spend as much time as possible with my sixth graders, all 47 of them. I looked forward to a parent stopping to see me after school. I even volunteered to supervise the high school detention room after school when some other sister had a conflict of time.

There was such a contrast of the light feeling in the classroom and the heavy feeling of the convent house.

Shortly after school began, it was apparent that Sister Superior had sized up the situation and had determined which sisters to berate and humiliate. For some reason, she began to pick on those sisters who were older, kind, and humble. It didn't matter whether it was night or day, in the convent house or in school. Sister found the smallest things to pick at. She would challenge them on the way they walked, the way they wore their habit, their tone of voice, anything she could think of.

It was particularly hard to witness this because the sisters involved continued to accept this harassment in a spirit of obedience. The vow of obedience required that we live the vow inwardly, as well as outwardly. My admiration swelled for those sweet sisters who cheerfully begged forgiveness for their infractions. They never questioned the penance imposed nor spoke about the unfairness of their treatment.

Many a time, during our quiet time in the community room, Sister Superior would berate one sister after the other, loudly telling them she was ashamed of them. She told them they didn't have control in their classrooms and that they were disgraceful teachers. None of this was true. I knew from the help they had given me that they were fine teachers.

I wanted to speak up so often, but knew it would be out of place.

I had to close the door of my classroom on occasions when Sister Superior would chastise one of these nuns in the school hallway. I know how embarrassed they must have felt and how humiliating this must have been for them. My heart ached.

One berated sister had been at this mission for 30 years and was an outstanding teacher. The sad part from my perspective was that this particular sister was a model nun. I looked on her as someone I wanted to emulate because she lived Holy Rule as I understood it.

One of the other sisters was an older nun, and a very capable teacher. I think she was one of the most generous, kind, and thoughtful persons I have ever met. It hurt so much to see her being picked on. Often I felt as if I wanted to do one of the penances for her.

On occasion Sister Superior would unexpectedly lash out at some of the other sisters for no apparent reason. If someone sneezed more than twice, she would be told to control herself because her sneezing was disgusting. Almost every morning this Superior would call attention to one of the younger nuns who couldn't get her veil on right.

After being reprimanded, these sisters often had to kneel in the doorway of a designated room in the convent house and recite several prayers out loud regardless of who was around. On occasion, these erring sisters had to stand during the next meditation period.

Somehow I remember having to stand during a meditation period. Whatever the infraction, it couldn't have been serious because I don't remember why I stood.

The hardest and most humiliating penance I remember, especially for the older sisters, was to eat their evening meal on their knees in the refectory.

Strange, but I thought it would be easier to live with all of this if Sister Superior had picked on me also. She never humiliated me publicly. Not once did she ever confront me. It probably was better that she didn't, because I don't believe I could have accepted that treatment in the same spirit in which those noble women did.

Now that doesn't mean I didn't have difficulty with this Superior. I did. Holy Rule had become a way of life for me that I accepted and respected. Sister Superior found a way to apply the rules to some people and not to others, particularly not to herself.

It was a common practice in our Order, that when we received a gift from anyone, be it a child, parent or relative, we would beg for it from our Superior.

When my parents came to visit every month or so, they'd bring me a box of goodies. Sometimes I received a package in the mail from my dad. My mother usually brought a couple of cakes or pies that I took to the kitchen immediately. I'd open other things gradually and we'd talk about them.

My dad would scout around for a special set of colored pencils, a new brand name pen, or a box of stationery to hint that I ought to write more often. My mother brought me lavender soap because she knew I liked the scent. She often brought lotions - one smelling better than the other. My folks got to be very good at surprising me with a variety of gifts.

My parents thought these gifts were for me and I never told them differently. Little did they know, that after their visit, I would haul my loot before the Superior, get on my knees and beg for one item.

"Sister Superior, I humbly beg to use this box of markers."

"Wouldn't you be more pleased with a smaller item?"

"Sister Superior, there is use for these markers in the sixth grade classroom."

It was important to watch my choice of words. We were not to accept ownership of anything, not even the classroom. I had to be careful not to say my classroom or to imply that these would be my markers. Most of the time I was able to keep the item I chose.

Because I was allowed to keep only one gift from their visit, it took me a while to decide which one I would beg for. I knew enough not to plan to keep the lavender soap or the sweet smelling lotions, because we were not allowed to use any items with a tantalizing scent.

Sister Superior told us not to discourage anyone from giving us gifts because the Motherhouse would be able to resell them. There was a large shipping box in a storage room to hold all of the extra gifts any sisters received. When the box was full, a parishioner driving to Milwaukee was asked to deliver it to the Motherhouse. A spacious gift shop was conveniently located near the visiting area in the Motherhouse.

I was content with the fate of my gifts. It was Holy Rule and I accepted it. The challenge inside of me came about because, the day after my parents would visit, I would see Sister Superior using the pen my dad brought or something else given to me. Some sisters, who were constantly fawning over the Superior, would flash a bottle of lotion identical to one my mother had just brought. None of this sat very well with me. I didn't want the items, but I didn't think others should have them either.

It didn't take much for me to be upset at anything Sister Superior did.

Between Thanksgiving and Christmas that year, I was beginning to see aspects of myself that I never knew existed. Why was I letting little things like this disturb me? What had happened to that beautiful life I

thought lay ahead of me?   What was wrong with me
that I was agonizing so much over everything I saw
happen under the new regime?

I came to terms with the fact that I was expected to
accept challenges. Life wasn't always going to be as I
thought it should be. People living outside the convent
didn't have things their way. Why did I think I should
be any different?

During the Christmas vacation I decided I would
change my attitude and make a fervent effort to see
some good in Sister Superior's actions. It seemed the
harder I tried, the more I was witness to her
inconsistencies in treatment of the nuns. The tirades
and verbal abuse were more prevalent than ever.

With our being together in the convent house day
after day, I could see we fit into three groups. There
were the fawners - trying to win grace in the Superior's
eyes. The humiliated ones - going about their duties
quietly setting a good example. And then there were
the observers - we did nothing to stop this.

Strong feelings of distrust consumed the observers.
No one felt free to trust even sisters who previously
had been friendly. It was as if every sister was suspect
of the other. No one knew who might distort what was
said and carry tales to the Superior. She needed no new
ammunition to fuel her attacks. We shared our
thoughts with no one. We had isolated ourselves as if
we were living alone.

I knew I wasn't the only one observing what was
happening. I realized that by not reacting to the abuse,
it was as if I condoned it. It was good we had no
mirrors in the house; I don't think I could have faced
myself. I couldn't find the reason why the sisters

professed longer than I didn't speak up. Could it be that they had seen this conduct before? Had they just hardened their hearts to it and were grateful they weren't in the receiving line?

So many nights I lie awake questioning, what is happening to my perfect life?

How much humiliation is one expected to accept in the name of obedience? I'm the third youngest professed in this house, why isn't someone older speaking up? Why am I seeing all this blatant meanness? Doesn't someone care? Sheer exhaustion eventually brought restless sleep.

What frightened me most were my waking thoughts. How could I stop Sister Superior? Speak up to her? Report her? Raise my hand to her? I never before entertained this type of thought directed to someone else. Sometimes I actually felt a fleeting urge to physically harm her.

With the coming of the New Year, I resolved to speak to someone of my dilemma. It was my only recourse. I had to speak to someone I could trust and be assured that what I said wouldn't get back to the Superior.

It was customary that everyone in religious life go to confession every week. The bishop of each diocese appointed a priest from a neighboring parish to be the confessor. A middle-aged priest, who lived in the city next to us, came each week.

Confession had become a rather rote process over the years. It seemed there was never anything worthwhile to confess. Acknowledgments like, I didn't help another sister when I knew I could be of assistance and had time to do it, would be the norm. I thought I was covering the situation when I confessed to having unkind thoughts about another.

For the next several weeks I laboriously poured out to Father my distress and confusion over what I saw and experienced. It was such a relief to finally be able to speak openly about my observations. Besides telling me to pray about it, Father gave suggestions to combat the upheaval I felt inside. He knew I wanted to salvage my religious calling. I prayed to every saint I ever heard of, hoping things would change.

Nothing changed.

There was a war going on inside of me. I worked so hard even to keep from wishing ill to Sister Superior. My thoughts toward her were turning more hurtful. I wanted to hurt her as she hurt others. The more she scorned the other sisters, the more evil were my thoughts of stopping her. If there had been a hole handy, I'd have wanted to shove her in.

It was apparent to me that Sister Superior's actions were affecting some of the other sisters as well. Even if they didn't create the negative feeling in our house or weren't responsible for the constant criticism, I saw their eyes swollen from crying. When I told Father I saw others crying, his only response was, "I know, I know. You must concentrate on your situation, not other's."

Gradually I felt confident enough to acknowledge to Father that I felt like a hypocrite. Here I was, wearing this beautiful habit, professing to be a bride of Christ, outwardly doing everything expected of me, but inwardly fighting a battle between good and evil.

We promised to live our vows of poverty, chastity and obedience, not just to the letter of Holy Rule, but from our hearts. Poverty and chastity were a snap. I lived the vow of obedience as the Rule specified, but in my heart I couldn't observe the spirit of obedience. Inwardly I was fighting Sister Superior all the way. Where was this going to end? What was I to do?

Father tried his best to convince me I could overcome these feelings and surrender my will to God through this Superior. He suggested that for the next six months I focus on the work at hand until school was over for the summer. In June I could ask for a transfer to a different mission.

I gave deep consideration to the idea that I make the next six months work. Except for Easter vacation, I knew I could keep myself very busy. I hoped I could find a way to get to the Motherhouse during the summer and speak directly with Reverend Mother to request a transfer.

However, my heart and mind gave me no rest. Maybe if I were transferred, everything would be fine for a time, but what about the future - five years, ten years? Would I be faced with a similar situation? I was 26 years old now, but how could I face myself if I lived like this again in 20 years? I certainly would never be true to myself or my Maker if I lived the life of a hypocrite. What was left for me to do?

In confession one day, Father asked me why I wanted to be a nun. I told him over and over I wanted nothing more than to live my life for God.

In a soft and gentle voice Father said, "Do you know you can live your life for God every day for the rest of your life outside the convent?"

I didn't know how to answer him.

Chapter Fifteen

Those next days were extremely difficult for me. I was afraid to think about what Father said, yet his words haunted me, because they echoed the deep question in my heart. I had given my life to God, could I just take it back? I had worked so hard to learn this life in the convent, to live this life and to love this life. Would that all have been wasted?

The following week I told Father I couldn't stop thinking about the prospect of leaving, but the whole concept frightened me. His words remain with me to this day, as if they were the words of God.

Father went on to explain that there are thousands of people in the world living a life pleasing to God. He said the convent was just one way. He asked me to call to mind the wonderful training I had received and how the quiet atmosphere gave me time to grow.

Father reminded me that I learned the importance of an education. I knew he was right. Had I stayed with my family, I never would have known that I could study and learn. Working with young children for the past seven years taught me the importance of nurturing, encouraging and respecting those little lives. Without the convent training, the education I received would never have been mine.

I remember Father saying, "You have been blessed with wonderful training, but you also gave ten years of your life to God in this special way." After a pause, he added, "Remember, you can live what you have learned out in the world as well as here."

I left the confessional that day totally confused. What would my leaving mean? What could I do? Where would I go? I would have to tell my parents, sisters and close relatives. Would they understand why I was leaving?

The following week I threw myself into my class work. During recreation I frequently found other tasks to occupy my time. I didn't feel like trying to have fun. I don't think I showed outwardly that I was troubled, because no one asked me if I was concerned about anything.

Periodically I would look down at my habit, with the rosary at my side. I couldn't picture myself not wearing the habit. This garb I cherished had become a part of me. The habit, the rosary and I were one; we were a package. I couldn't leave it all behind.

Time didn't move fast enough for the next time to go to confession. Things had not changed in the convent house. My thoughts about Sister Superior had not improved. I knew I had to make a decision and soon.

At my next confession I told Father I thought maybe I had to leave, but didn't want to.

Father said, "Perhaps you are ready to lead a life for God out in the world. The same guidance, protection and love you found in the convent can be yours in the world."

I didn't want to hear that, but it felt right inside me. I felt as if the bottom dropped out of my existence. Had these ten years been a preparation for what was to take place the rest of my life? How did I even dare consider leaving this haven I had found?

Father suggested that during the coming week, I make a fervent effort to place my concerns before God and totally surrender the outcome to Him. He said to repeat often, "Not my will, but Thine be done."

I didn't want to make a decision just yet, but I did notice that I felt lighter. I almost had a sense of relief. An option was at hand. I prayed for guidance and certainty.

The next time Father came, I told him I had decided to leave. He assured me that either staying or leaving was pleasing to God.

"If we really love God," he said, "it doesn't matter where we are."

Father laughed when I said, "Then I won't go to hell for this?"

His laugh made me laugh.

"It's high time you start to laugh," he chuckled and added, "Call the Bishop tomorrow. Let him know of your decision."

"Father," I said, "Our Order is a Papal Order and I have to write to Rome to be released from my vows."

His quick response was, "Then call the Motherhouse and ask them what the procedure is. I'm sure it's very simple."

I waited a couple of days to make the call. What would I say? For whom would I ask? Prior to this, no one knew what I was considering. What would Sister Superior do or say when she found out? I didn't want my fellow sisters to know. Was I strong enough within myself to face this step?

Finally, I got the courage to call the Motherhouse. When a sister answered the phone, I blurted out, "I'm leaving the convent and want to know how to write to Rome."

I think I took the sister by surprise because she timidly said, "Just hold on a minute."

In a moment or two, another sister identified herself as part of the Provincialate, those sisters who ran the Order in America, and said, "Now what is this all about?"

I told her who I was and that I was leaving the convent. I needed to know how to write to Rome. With a stern voice, she asked my address and said she would send the papers.

Chapter Sixteen

Within a week an envelope arrived addressed to me marked confidential. It was customary in the Order for the Sister Superior to open all mail before giving it to any of us. Sister Superior didn't open this envelope before she gave it to me. I could tell from her hesitation in placing it in my hand that she wanted to know why I was getting a letter from the Motherhouse.

I merely said, "Thank you, Sister Superior," and walked away. It amused me to keep her guessing.

That weekend I filled out the enclosed forms. I was required to attach a hand written request to the Holy Father explaining why I asked for release from my vows. My confessor had told me ahead of time to briefly explain the upheaval I was feeling within myself. He said to add the statement that it was my intent to lead an honorable life as a layperson.

*   *   *

This was 1951, long before the great exodus in the early 1960s of men and women leaving the sisterhood and monastic life. At the time I left, there was a stigma about leaving the convent or priesthood among Christians, especially Catholics. Many felt it was an act of turning away from God and the breaking of a vow.

Let me clarify the misconception about religious vows. Many lay people believed that a final vow required the nun to stay in the convent for the rest of her life. The truth was rather the opposite. The sister was in fact, guaranteed a home for life. This protected her in the event she needed long-term care as a result of contracting a serious illness such as tuberculosis or emotional problems. The head of the Order was also free to dismiss anyone before final vows who demonstrated any type of misconduct.

The laity didn't understand that most Orders, mine included, required that the novices pronounce their vows two times for three years. The first three years and the second three years were a period of probation. Prior to final vows, a sister could be denied renewal of vows or sent home at any time.

Final vows expressed an intention to stay for life, but in no way required the nun to stay. It was common knowledge that Papal Canon Law stated that with the permission of Rome, any nun was free to leave without jeopardizing her relationship with the Church.

Because of these misconceptions, those who left religious life were often isolated from others and filled with guilt. Add that to the fact that the real world brought unfamiliar challenges after a life where virtually every move was directed from a rulebook. Basics like housing, food and maintenance were often daunting responsibilities. Unfortunately, many who left religious life felt driven away from the church by their guilt and wound up in undesirable relationships or alcoholism.

*   *   *

I read and reread all the forms and my written request many times before sealing the envelope. I made sure I put my return address on the envelope, but wasn't sure how to get some stamps. When no one was around, I called the post office to find out the rate for overseas mail. After I was asked how many sheets there were in the envelope, the postman told me how many stamps to attach.

I didn't have any money to purchase stamps, nor would I have been able to go to the post office. I stepped out of character a little bit when I stole enough stamps out of Sister Superior's desk when no one was around.

On February 9, 1951 without hesitation, I dropped the envelope in the mailbox on the corner of the church property. The die was cast.

I never found out if Sister Superior knew of my intention. It was obvious to me the other sisters in our house knew nothing of what was going on.

My next step was to alert my parents that I'd be coming home at the end of the school term. That letter was probably more difficult to write than filling out the forms and writing the Papal request. I had no intention of going into any explanation about my feelings for Sister Superior. My folks wouldn't have believed me anyhow.

Nuns and priests in my parents' eyes were saints, except for me. Perhaps my dad would have believed me, but not my mother. I don't recall the words, but I know I told them I decided it was the right thing for me to leave. To help them understand, I told them I had the blessing of my confessor. That was the only consolation I could give them.

Because I had no secular clothes to change into, I asked my mom to please bring a dress, stockings, underclothes and shoes to wear the next time they came to visit.

My parents never came again, but my Mother sent a box. No letters came from them either. I knew they felt shame.

There were four months of school left. I wanted to enjoy every minute. The children and I worked well together. Many of my sixth-grade boys participated in the regional basketball tournament. Having a high school, as well as the grade school, we had a large enough gymnasium and could play host. I was able to root for our team at many of the games after school.

In the classroom I made every project we worked on something special, because I knew this was the last time for me. Every so often one of the youngsters would say something like, "We want to come back to see you next year and let you know how we're doing." I'd always say, "That's a great idea." I knew I was going to miss them and teaching very much.

To this day, every September, I remember the excitement of new children entering the classroom. The month of June always brings a little tug to my heart. I recall the pain of loss I experienced when my students left for the summer each year.

I was sure the message of my leaving had reached Reverend Mother in the Motherhouse. About the

second week of March, Sister Superior announced
Reverend Mother was coming to visit our convent
house. She told us that whenever Reverend Mother
visited a mission, it was customary for her to interview
each sister starting with the one who had professed
vows the longest. The news of Mother's visit created a
buzz.

It was out of the ordinary that Reverend Mother
would visit a mission. If a parish had a big
commemorative celebration, a representative of the
Motherhouse might attend, but to hear out of the blue
that Mother herself was coming was very unusual.

I heard one sister say to another, "Do you think
Superior told Mother bad things about us?" Many of
the sisters were really concerned. I began to wonder if
they felt guilty about something.

When I was asked what I thought, my usual
response was, "I don't know, but Mother must have a
reason." I knew the reason she was coming, but no one
was going to hear it from me.

Reverend Mother arrived. She was gracious and
friendly to all of us. At dinner the first evening, she
suspended the spiritual reading. It seemed like
Christmas or Easter now.

Normally we talked at meals only on holidays. No
encouragement was needed to get us to start talking up
a storm. We enjoyed our dinner as we laughed and
visited with each other.

Recreation that night was rather subdued. Everyone
was hesitant to get the cards or board games out.
Maybe secretly, Mother wished to join in our usual fun
time, but I think we wanted to make a good impression
on her. To me, we looked rather silly sitting in a large

group, hands in our big sleeves trying to carry on intelligent discussions. I'm sure Mother recognized we weren't being our real selves.

This Reverend Mother was not the sister we had as Superior the first three years. After that sister's three-year term, another sister was elected Reverend Mother of the Order. I had never socialized with this Reverend Mother before.

The next day was Saturday and interviews began after breakfast. There were 20 nuns ahead of me for an interview, so my call came Sunday afternoon. I didn't know what to expect. I wasn't afraid to talk with Mother, but I did think she would reprimand me for being so bold as to consider leaving.

Reverend Mother smiled as I entered the parlor. There was a desk set up for her in the room. I sat in a chair set to the side of the desk. She couldn't have been sweeter. She began by reiterating all the things I had done those seven years. Mother told me that the other sisters had nice things to say about me. She thanked me for having been willing to take on that extra large class of 72 children when the other sister became ill. Mother commented on a thank you note sent to the Motherhouse from St. Norbert College about the Gregorian chant class. I had no idea she knew so many things about me.

Then came the big question. "Why, my dear, are you considering leaving our Order?"

I began by telling Mother I enjoyed being Sister Marcele and sincerely loved and respected Holy Rule. Mother listened silently as I went on about how rewarding it was to be a teacher. She told me she also loved those years. I could see in her eyes how she was remembering what it felt like to be in a classroom.

"Things are different for me now," she said. "My responsibilities these days are often heavy in comparison to the delight of being in a classroom." A serious look crossed her face as she said, "Why then are you considering leaving?"

"Mother, I am not able to live the spirit of my vow of obedience." I told her I could not tolerate the abuse of Sister Superior. I explained that none of the ranting was ever directed at me, but I felt it was unjustly imposed on other sisters. I added that I felt Sister Superior considered Holy Rule was for us and not for her.

"Mother, I recognize this is my failing and not anybody else's."

Reverend Mother must have heard enough from the sisters ahead of me; she didn't seem surprised at anything I said. The words just kept running out of my mouth. I tried to explain that I felt such a burning in my chest – such anger towards Sister Superior. With a feeling of shame, I added that I had to confess actually wanting sometimes to physically hurt her.

Reverend Mother put my hands in hers, looked pleadingly into my eyes and said, "You are considered an exemplary nun. We don't want you to leave. In a few years you will be a Superior yourself." She went on to say that if I'd stay till the end of the school year, she would transfer me to another mission even before summer school.

I interjected, "I plan to stay to the end of the school year, Reverend Mother. These are my children."

I didn't know if Reverend Mother knew, so I told her I had already mailed my request to Rome. She was taken aback by that comment and tears came to her eyes.

"I came hoping you would change your mind," she said.

Her kindness touched me. We both had tears to wipe away.

To this day I don't know where I got the strength to tell Reverend Mother there was no turning back for me. I explained to her that I might be transferred to a wonderful mission, but the day was bound to come when I again couldn't live the spirit of the vow. The older I would be, the harder the transition to secular living.

After our interview, she blessed me and wished me well.

Chapter Seventeen

When I left the room I felt as if I had to be by myself for a while. The experience had been emotionally draining. On my way to the chapel I stopped in the community room to check something in the dictionary. I had never heard the word "exemplary" before. I was very touched when I read that it meant serving as a pattern and deserving of imitation.

The chapel was empty. I sat in my usual place and mentally reviewed what had just transpired in the interview. I appreciated the graciousness of Reverend Mother and was humbled to think she wanted me to stay. As a sense of peace gradually came over me, I felt relief knowing I had made the right decision.

During the early part of June our classes ended and the children were on their way. We had a couple of days to prepare our classroom for the major cleaning of the school during the summer. Also the children's records had to be updated for their next teacher. I remember well the day I left my classroom for the last time.

Most of the teaching sisters received assignments for attending summer school. I received none. The older sisters usually didn't request summer assignments. Only a few sisters noticed that I wasn't preparing to leave.

When asked about it, I would say, "I don't plan to go to summer school this year."

They didn't question me further nor did they even seem to care. There were nine sisters left with me at our mission for the summer.

It seemed strange for only nine of us to be in this big house while everyone else was away for the summer. The regular housework, dusting, sweeping, cleaning the bathrooms was much easier with fewer nuns in the house. I knew enough not to be underfoot of the cook, so I spent time each day helping the laundress. I was better off keeping myself busy because it was hard to concentrate on reading and thinking only made me worry.

It was more fun to wait on and pamper the four older sisters too. I polished their shoes and washed out their stockings. They were kind to me and never asked why I didn't leave for summer school with the other sisters. If they suspected I was leaving, they never verbalized it.

The music sister chose not to go away for the summer. It was fun to have my Aggie around. I had befriended her when others shunned her because of her peculiar ways. Typical of many artists, Sister was very childlike and often appeared to live on a cloud all her own. It was easy for Sister Superior to make fun of her and humiliate her during the year.

Aggie was the only one left who enjoyed playing cards and games. We didn't have to adhere to the strict rule of silence during the day so, when chores were done, there was time for relaxation and games.

Being the youngest in the household, I played the role of portress, answering the doors, taking telephone messages, putting groceries away as they arrived - anything that needed to be done. I waited patiently every day for the mailman to come, hoping that each day my release papers would arrive.

On entering one of the storage rooms one day, I was surprised to see the laundress packing a trunk. I asked her if she was leaving. Rather joyfully, she told me she had been instructed to pack up Sister Superior's clothes and send the trunk to the Motherhouse. Sister Superior was not off teaching summer school as she had explained to us. Her summer assignment was instead to return to the Motherhouse.

"Sister wasn't permitted to come back to the mission to gather her things," the laundress said.

Inwardly I was pleased to know that Reverend Mother meant it when she had told me she would take care of our situation.

The third week, when Father came, I told him about Sister Superior not returning and how I hadn't received any papers from Rome. He assured me they certainly must be on their way and told me to be ready to go when the time came.

The following week, when I saw Father, he suggested I call the Motherhouse and inquire about the papers. That afternoon I called and asked to speak to someone in the Provincialate. I could tell I was speaking to the same sister who said she would send the forms to me in February.

She said, "Why haven't you come to the Motherhouse? We've been waiting for you. You must wait here until the papers arrive."

I was taken by surprise and said, "Nobody told me to come."

"Request the money from the sister in charge over the summer and get in here." With that she hung up the phone.

That evening I called Father to tell him what had transpired. He was very upset and told me, "You're not going there. They'll never let you out."

My only response was, "Father, I don't know what to do. I'm so confused."

"Now don't you worry, I'm going to take care of everything," Father said. He explained he would call me the following evening. I felt very uneasy about all of this. I really didn't know why he didn't want me to go to the Motherhouse. He never explained.

I wondered how all of this would end. I wanted to leave in the manner prescribed by Canon Law. I notified the Motherhouse, wrote to Rome as directed, so why wasn't this being resolved?

A friend of mine from our Order just walked out the front door of the convent one day without notifying anyone. I thought to myself, she's fine and hasn't experienced any recrimination. I knew this because she was living in a nearby community and stopped to see me on occasion after school in my classroom.

I think it was because I trusted Father, that I decided to wait until I heard from him again. It was difficult not having anyone else to talk to about this. I felt so alone in the world those days.

The following evening, Father called to tell me he contacted the Canonical Visitator of the Diocese, who lived in Green Bay. I had never heard of him before. Father explained that this priest was appointed by the Bishop to oversee the religious members of the Diocese. He served as champion of both men and women in religious orders, as well as to serve as disciplinarian when needed. Father had explained my situation to this priest and told him that because my papers had not arrived, I'd been told to go to the Motherhouse.

The Canonical Visitator emphatically said I was not to go to the Motherhouse. He said he would check further and make inquiry about the release papers. Father said he'd call me when he had any news.

On the Fourth of July, the cook sister prepared a picnic lunch for us to enjoy outside. It wasn't a fun day for me because I had so much on my mind. I wanted to be gone before the sisters came back from summer school. It appeared as if my stay here would just drag on.

A few days later Father called to tell me he had spoken with the Canonical Visitator, who had checked with the Papal Nuncio in Washington, DC. The Papal Nuncio has direct contact with the Vatican. He learned my papers had been sent to the Motherhouse the first week of April, three months earlier. Father suggested I again call the Motherhouse and request the papers be sent to our mission.

The following morning I called the Motherhouse, even though I didn't want to speak to anyone there anymore. The same unfriendly sister answered the phone. I explained I found out my papers had been at the Motherhouse since April and would she please forward them to our mission.

All she said was, "I have nothing to say to you other than come to the Motherhouse." That ended the phone connection, and I hung up too.

That evening after dinner, I called Father to relay my morning conversation with the sister in the Motherhouse. Even talking to Father was difficult for me now. The last few times we spoke on the phone, it was hard for me not to cry. I had so much pent-up emotion, which I couldn't show when I was with the sisters. Father was very kind and always reassured me that everything would be fine.

"Just ignore the way sister talked to you on the phone. She has no claim on you," Father said. He added that he'd be in touch with me soon.

The days passed very slowly. Aggie, the music sister, played and I still sang the morning Mass in church. I believe I prayed harder those days than ever before. I didn't want to stay, and at the same time, I didn't want to go home. I knew my parents would feel disgraced at my leaving the convent, even if I was honorably released from my vows. Sometimes I felt as if it was more than I could cope with.

Every week when Father came for confession, he told me not to worry and that everything would be resolved and done properly. I really don't think he knew how this was going to turn out, but his positive and reassuring words kept me going.

The last week of July, when Father came for confession, he told me the Canonical Visitator had again been in touch with the Papal Nuncio. The Vatican would be contacted and a clear determination made regarding my leaving. I didn't know if that was good or bad, but Father seemed to be pleased about the news.

Father's last words were, "See that you are ready."

During dinner, four or five days later, the phone rang and I left the table to answer. It was Father. He began by telling me the Holy Father sends blessings.

"Are you kidding me? Did the Pope really bless me?

"I wouldn't have said it if I hadn't been told to tell you. Now stop crying and listen to me."

Father went on to explain that according to the Papal Nuncio, relayed to Father by the Canonical Visitator, I had permission to leave my mission without papers. The Motherhouse would be directed to contact me later and provide an opportunity to sign the papers.

I could hardly catch my breath. "This is it. I am free to go?" I asked.

Father said, "Are you ready to leave tonight?"

"Not tonight Father, I have to adjust to the news. Tomorrow will be fine after night prayer. I'll go to 7:00 p.m. prayer and be ready shortly after 8:00."

Father told me, "I'll pick you up at that time tomorrow night and take you to the home of one of my parishioners. We'll talk about your going home to Milwaukee then."

I was in a daze when I hung up the phone.

I returned to the dining table and tried to finish my meal. I'm not sure if my face was a dead giveaway or if I had done something to spark Aggie's inquiry. When we left the dining room, she pulled me aside and made sure we were out of earshot of the others.

"Marcie, are you going over the wall?"

I'm not sure if it was her intuition, or something I said or did that prompted her to ask me. Her words did amuse me though. I remembered we heard of a book or movie about a woman who left the convent using the words "going over the wall." Aggie had such a pained expression on her face and tears in her eyes that I knew she deserved some kind of answer.

All I could say was "Aggie, I won't be here tomorrow night."

She took hold of my hands and holding them firmly said, "Please take me with you. I'll work for you for the rest of my life. I'll take good care of you. I won't be a bother ever."

"You must have family to call on. I can't take you with me. We have to do this through Rome. Have you ever spoken to your family about this?" I said.

"I have a brother older than I. He said he has no room for me. I have no place to go if I leave here. I would work for you for the rest of my life – really!"

I felt sorry for her. I was concerned about her myself. Granted she was only in her 50s, but she needed someone to take care of her. These past years I had been supportive of her and I know she relied on me for so many things. I worried about what would happen to her after I was gone.

"Aggie," I said, "The angels will take good care of you. Please don't talk about this to anyone, but I am leaving tomorrow with the permission of Rome."

Father had said not to talk about this, but I had to say something to her. If the other sisters knew, they might alert the Motherhouse and be instructed to confine me. Anyhow, I didn't need undue pressure from anyone.

"Don't go," she repeated, "Don't go."

"I have to. Everything is arranged. I'm to leave tomorrow."

We hugged for a moment and then Aggie went into the chapel. Recreation had begun before I walked into the community room.

A few of the sisters were busy knitting. I looked at new patterns with them, but felt out of place.

I went to the kitchen and surprised the cook sister by offering to dry dishes for her. That was not my habit.

At 7:00 p.m. the bell rang and I went to early night prayer. I drank in the vision of the chapel. I didn't want to forget how it looked. There was so much going on in my mind, it was hard to pray.

I lay in bed that night trying to remember everything I wanted to take care of during my last day there.

My final thoughts of the night were about the Pope blessing me. I took that gesture as an assurance that I was doing the right thing and that the Holy Father himself concurred. I was reassured that my leaving was meant to be.

It was hard to keep busy that last day on mission. I quietly emptied my desk, putting all the supplies into the storage room. When putting books I had been using back on the shelves, I straightened and arranged every book in order. Everything I did that day had a strange finality to it. Much of my time was spent with the laundress, in order to avoid being around the other sisters.

Time was moving slowly for me. I found myself frequently in the Chapel that day, thanking God for the strength to see this transition through. This included expressing gratitude for the caring Priest overseeing all the details. I reaffirmed my promise of dedication to God even though I'd be outside the convent.

During the afternoon I realized I hadn't seen Aggie all day. She seemed to have disappeared after breakfast. I asked the cook sister if she knew where Sister was. She told me she had taken some lunch up to her, but Aggie had refused it. Mid-afternoon I went up to her room and knocked on her door. Aggie told me to go away. No amount of persuasion could make her open the door.

She said, "It's easier for me not to see you at all. Just leave me alone."

At dinner that evening, I offered to do the spiritual reading. I felt more at ease sitting over to the side of those eating, rather than at the dinner table with them. I noticed Aggie had not joined us. We said our prayer after the meal, and the sisters left the room. I sat quietly with my meal, not hurrying. I wasn't eager to join the others in recreation. I knew I was leaving right after first night prayer.

*   *   *

My mind turned again to what was really going on. It was time to bring my awareness back to the task at hand. I was in the process of leaving the convent. Having mounted the stairs after night prayer, I had entered my cell for the last time. I placed my religious garb neatly on the bed.

I picked up my copy of Holy Rule, my breviary and the manual of prayers. The manual contained sections used for specific group praying, especially in the morning and at night. It included the prayers we said to ourselves as we put on each piece of our garb each day. These three books were all treasures. I wanted to take them with me, but they weren't mine.

I placed the books on the bed next to the habit. Now I had no Holy Rule book to guide me anymore. The breviary had become so much a part of every day. How was I going to honor the various hours of the day without it? I knew I would miss the soft leather cover of the manual of prayers. I had begun and ended every day with it for eight years.

I kept asking myself, why is this so hard? I had been looking forward to this day and now that it's here, I'm afraid. I felt so alone. My life would be different now. I determined I was going to be strong and learn to fit into the outside world.

I realized at this point I had better hurry. It would soon be eight o'clock.

Before taking off my slip, I reached under the bed to retrieve the box my mother sent me. I purposely kept it sealed so no one would see its contents and conclude that I was leaving. It was easy to tell from the size of the box, it didn't hold shoes. Horror came over me when I saw what it did contain. My mother had sent what we called years ago, a wash dress or a housedress and a pair of white ankle socks. There was no slip, no under clothes, no stockings. I knew she wasn't eager for me to come home, but how would she expect that I could manage with this?

The dress was so thin you could actually see the light through it. I had to have a slip. The only alternative I had was to cut the lower portion off the one I was wearing. I wanted to sit down and cry, but there just wasn't time. I cut the bottom of the slip off. The first time around I left it too long. Time was slipping by. I had to cut around again. I put on the shortened slip and then the dress.

Oh what a sight! The material of the dress had big flowers on it and was at least a size too big. It just hung on me.

All of a sudden I realized something that had not come to my mind before. This was the first time in ten and a half years that so much of my body was uncovered. In the candidature we wore long dresses with long sleeves. Since the novitiate, only my face and hands had been exposed. I looked down at myself gawking at my arms, because the dress had short sleeves.

My legs were sticking out from the bottom of the dress. I felt my neck and my hair. Since February, when I sent the papers to Rome, I had let my hair grow. It covered my ears, but was so uneven at the bottom. All these years I had cut it short enough to wear the wimple comfortably.

I felt positively naked. How was I ever going to get used to this?

I sat down and put the anklets on. The only choice available to me was to put on my black, heavy shoes. I was glad there was no mirror in the room, but what was Father going to say when he saw me? I could just imagine the shocked look on my parents' face if they saw me like this. I couldn't take a train home in this condition.

What was going to become of me?

I glanced at the little clock mounted on the top of the dresser. It was four minutes to eight. I certainly wasn't going to walk through the corridor and down the stairway to the back door looking like this. If I hadn't known inside myself that it was right for me to leave, I don't believe I physically could have even considered leaving the room. I decided to put on my bathrobe over the dress. I reached for a white scarf and put it on. We normally wore one over our heads at night when we left our room to go to the bathroom.

The little clock indicated there was just one minute left. I looked over the room once more and rested my eyes on the habit and books that lay on the bed. It was time to go. I took a deep breath, turned out the light, opened the door, and then stopped. As if by instinct, I walked back and tucked the manual of prayers under my arm, then left the room and closed the door behind me.

With eyes cast down, I walked the length of the corridor and down the stairs to the back door. I took off the bathrobe, dropped it and the white scarf on the floor, opened the back door and walked to the car.

Chapter Eighteen

I was very self-conscious when glancing at myself sitting in the car. Timidly I greeted Father. The summer sky was not dark enough at 8:00 p.m. to hide my appearance. I explained that these were the clothes sent to me and I had nothing else to put on.

I felt Father wanted to laugh, but was too polite to do that. Surely no one in his parish ever looked like I did. Looking down at myself I saw so much skin. There were no big sleeves to hide my arms or a long skirt to cover my legs. I was very uncomfortable.

Certainly I would've felt more at ease if it were my own father picking me up rather than a priest. My parents didn't want anything to do with this exodus, so I was grateful for the help.

"Don't worry about a thing," Father said. "We'll go over to Mrs. Murray's house and talk this all over. I want you to stay there for a day or two before you go home to Milwaukee."

"She has room for me?"

"There are rooms to rent, but you would be a guest. She's eager to have you come. Mrs. Murray told me you had her grandson in your class for several grades."

My heart dropped. I was hoping I would be with people who didn't know me or know I had just come from the convent. As I thought it over, anyone taking a good look at me would have a hard time deciding what planet I flew in from. Thoughts were running through my mind as to what I would say to Mrs. Murray when I met her. Worse yet, I wondered what she would think of me.

When we arrived, Father rang the doorbell. Mrs. Murray answered the door with a smile, eagerly ushering us into her living room. Here was a widowed woman in her mid-60s making us feel right at home.

She said, "I've been waiting all day for you to come," as she placed a tray of assorted desserts on her coffee table. She hurried back to the kitchen and returned with a pot of coffee and some cups.

Father said to Mrs. Murray, "You have a daughter that lives nearby, don't you?" Before Mrs. Murray had a chance to answer, Father continued, "Would you mind giving her a call and asking her to come over here? I think maybe she can do a little shopping for us."

Mrs. Murray bounced up and walked to the phone. "I'll call her. She'll be here right away."

I could tell from the way the conversation was going that all of this had been planned before my arrival. After the call, Mrs. Murray told me who her daughter was. I remembered that I had her son in second and in sixth grade. She had accompanied us on field trips, so I knew very well who she was. My next hope was that I would not have to see her son.

We passed the time with light conversation until Mrs. Murray's daughter, Sandy, walked in. I'm sure she had been prepped not to make a big issue of where I had come from.

Father said, "I think you know Shirley. She's going to stay with your Mother a couple days."

Sandy spoke as if I looked the same way I had when she'd drop in at school. I have to admit, they all tried their best to put me at ease.

We enjoyed the treats and the small talk continued. I didn't talk very much because I still was overwhelmed at what I had done. I just walked out of the convent! Why am I here?

After a short while, Father stood up and handed Sandy some money saying, "Give Shirley a permanent in the morning and take her shopping. We can't send her home looking like this. Find what she needs for a couple days. See that she gets some shoes."

Father thanked both women and turned to me saying, "You'll be fine. Just wait and see."

As Father walked to the door, Mrs. Murray invited him for dinner the next evening.

My two new friends took me to the room I would occupy. Mrs. Murray pointed to a pair of pajamas on the bed and said, "These are from us for you to keep. Sleep tight."

With that, they closed the door as they left the room.

What a beautiful room! The bed had a pretty, light blue cover with ruffles all around it. Attractive curtains graced the windows. There was a radio, a phonograph and an upholstered chair in the room. A bookshelf, an end table, and nightstand had doilies and pretty little things on them. Compared to our bare cells in the convent, this was like a room in a mansion. Everything will be so different from now on, I thought.

I cried when I looked at myself in the mirror over the dresser. This can't be what I really look like, flashed through my mind. How am I going to fit into the world again?

I put on the pajamas they left for me. The last time I put pajamas on I was still living at home. So much had happened since those days. I had been living my dream as a nun and now that was no more.

That night I lie in bed wondering what lay ahead for me. If only I didn't have to face my parents. What will my sisters and their families in Milwaukee think of me? Will I teach or get a regular job? With my hair the way it was, how could Sandy give me a perm? If we shop tomorrow, what will it feel like if I go into a store? I hadn't been in one for ten years. Just plain fear blinded me.

A soft breeze and the sunshine were playing with the curtains when I awoke the next morning. It startled me when I realized all of this was not a dream.

I am really in Mrs. Murray's home.

I reached for the manual of prayers I had brought with me in order to say my morning prayers, but decided to just make up a prayer of my own.

After dressing, I went downstairs and found I was an early riser.

Before long, Mrs. Murray came down and whipped up a hearty breakfast. Sandy came over and set the plans for the day as we enjoyed our meal. No one read to us, we just talked.

Sandy had brought the things along to give me a permanent, so that was first on the list.

My hair had not been styled or cut carefully all these past two years. My old roommate, my friendly barber, had been transferred to another mission.

Sandy gave me a trim and washed my hair over the bathroom sink as my mother had done years ago when I was young.

Memory of previous perms had escaped me. I had forgotten the smell of the solution used, or the winding of the little curlers that had to be done. It wasn't comfortable while we had to wait for the curl to set. Funny, I remembered a saying my mother often used, "Vanity must suffer."

With my hair not very long, I assumed I'd look silly as a curly top. After the hair was dried and combed, both women told me I looked very nice. I felt better than I had the night before.

Following a light lunch, Sandy and I ventured out and found a pair of shoes to buy. I wore them out of the store. We hid the convent shoes in a bag as we continued on our way.

The next stop was a department store. It was so big. There were many people bustling around shopping. I had forgotten what it would feel like being in a store after all these years. The sounds, the sight of so much merchandise, the smell, all of this made me violently ill. I told Sandy we had to get out of there.

We walked up and down the street for a while. I told Sandy that years ago I went shopping with my mother and it never bothered me. We concluded this happened because I had not been in any type of public place for so many years.

Sandy said we'd start slowly. She decided we had better settle for just a dress shop instead of a department store. I convinced myself that everything would be fine and it was. After trying on several outfits, we chose two and an extra blouse. Again, I wore something new out of the store.

We went to a lingerie shop for a few needs and then found a drugstore. Sandy told me that was the best spot to find reasonably priced makeup.

We found our way back to Mrs. Murray's house to show off our purchases. Before Sandy left, she did my makeup.

I had no idea how much money Father gave Sandy. It never occurred to me to even ask. I had no concept of money. In the convent when anything was needed, we went to the Superior, knelt down and begged for it. It didn't matter if we requested a bar of soap, a pair of stockings or a new pair of shoes.

In the convent we never handled money or had any of our own. Monthly, the parish secretary would give a $40 check to Sister Superior for each of the teaching sisters. With that, she managed our needs.

Later, when Mrs. Murray was busy in the kitchen, I found a full-length mirror. I didn't recognize myself. My appearance was presentable, but I wasn't sure I liked what I saw. There stood a worldly woman. It was as if I had a costume on and was playing a role. Could I ever be just me, dressed like this?

When Father came that evening, Mrs. Murray had prepared a feast for our enjoyment. The three of us chatted, but I had difficulty following the conversation. I was confused about what I had seen in the mirror.

After dinner, Father said he would like to have a little talk with me. He and I went into the living room, as Mrs. Murray busied herself clearing the table and doing the dishes.

Father again told me how nice I looked. He said all of this change will just take time. I was to be patient and be myself.

I told him I didn't know the woman I saw in the mirror. I said, "I don't know who I am."

Father went on to explain that inside, I was the same person I had always been. He said he knew me to be a woman of character who wanted to live her life for God. He stressed that it doesn't matter what the outside garb is, but who we are.

I knew what Father meant and I agreed with him. Strange, I knew I liked me when I was a nun, but I didn't know if I liked me now. I was very grateful he didn't say I was to go back to Milwaukee the next day. I knew I wasn't ready to face my parents.

Before Father left, he told me to be at peace and to sleep well. He reminded me that Sandy said she'd be back the next day. "Enjoy yourself; be sure and have a good time," Father said. After saying goodbye to Mrs. Murray, he told her he would stop back the next evening.

It felt good to sleep in a little bit the second morning. It was surprising to see 7:30 on the clock. Rising time had been 5:00 a.m. all those years. It almost felt scandalous sitting in the upholstered chair to say my prayers and meditate. I realized I wouldn't be kneeling so much anymore. It frightened me to think of all the changes ahead.

After showering and getting dressed, I went downstairs to find Mrs. Murray busy in the kitchen. I felt so at home with her and wanted to see what I could do to help. Mrs. Murray liked to talk and I enjoyed the freedom of being able to chat with her as much as I cared to. It was strange not to have a loud bell summoning me to go here or there.

Three places were set at the table, and as expected, Sandy joined us for breakfast. She said she had a few errands to run and thought I might like to join her. She also offered to drive around a beautiful lake nearby that I hadn't seen before.

Mrs. Murray said she had several things to do around the house and we should go without her. The plan was that we would stop back and pick her up around noon. They planned to take me to one of their favorite restaurants about 35 miles away.

Sandy and I took off for the post office, picked up some clothes from the cleaners, and made our way to a five and dime store. I had forgotten all about that type of store. We had so much fun. The store had many inexpensive items. We tried on sunglasses, and draped several varieties of narrow scarves and billowy scarves around our necks. We even perched all kinds of sun hats on our heads. Sandy bought me some beautiful thank you cards, because I wanted one for Father and one for Mrs. Murray.

Our ride around the lake was lovely. I had forgotten the beauty of a serene lake surrounded by trees and free growing greenery. There were some homes fairly close to the water. We could see people sitting outside sunning themselves and children having fun playing. I had forgotten about the outside world. Not everyone was living their life as I had, and that was fine.

After picking up Mrs. Murray, we drove to the restaurant. On the way there they asked if I had ever eaten lobster tail. When I responded that I hadn't, they told me I was in for a big treat.

Just stepping into the restaurant was an experience in itself. We entered through very beautiful high doors with stained glass. A well-dressed uniformed man greeted us kindly and took us to a table by a window. I had a wonderful view of the dining room and outside the window I saw a little pond graced with water lilies.

Mrs. Murray ordered some wine that we shared and placed our dinner orders. We clued her in on what we had done during the morning. After our food arrived, Sandy showed me how to take the meat out of the lobster shell with a little fork I hadn't seen before. I never imagined how delicious lobster could taste dipped in butter.

What I remember most about this experience was observing the people at the other tables. The restaurant was crowded and all the people in little groups were living out the script of their own lives. No one was taking note of me. I found I didn't have a little sign hanging around my neck saying, "I am an ex-nun." It was then I knew I didn't have to be afraid to be out in public.

Father stopped by in the evening to hear the tales of the day. I could tell by his smile he was pleased that all went well.

He said, "See Shirley, I told you everything would be fine. You're doing very well, even better than I expected."

As Father turned to Sandy he questioned, "Does it still work out all right for you to take Shirley to Milwaukee tomorrow?"

Father's words confirmed what I had already expected. It was obvious to me that all of this had been discussed prior to my even leaving the convent. I could tell they all knew what role they were playing in this whole experience. My assumption had been that I would just take the train back to Milwaukee. I was very grateful because all of this sounded so much easier.

"Yes, Father, "Sandy said, "The car is ready and my family will be okay."

"Father, do you really think I'm ready?" I said. "I don't want to go home. I told you how my folks feel about all this." In my heart I knew I'd be lost without the support of Father, Mrs. Murray and Sandy. A feeling of aloneness crept over me.

"I plan to call your folks early tomorrow morning. I'm sure they'll be pleased to know you'll be coming home."

I thought to myself, *if you only knew*.

It was then I was reminded of a quote that impressed me some time ago. "It isn't gravity itself that binds, but the gravity of limited thinking." I knew I had to pull myself together and rely on the strong faith I grew up with. I had made a decision, knew it to be right, and therefore all I had to do was trust that I'd be guided.

Father sensed my dilemma. "What you already have done required strength," he said. "There is no reason to think you don't have the strength to face anything that presents itself -- especially seeing your parents and family." Smiling he added, "Everything will be fine."

Sandy got up to leave. After saying goodbye to everyone, her mother suggested she stop over for an early lunch the next day before we left. Mrs. Murray also left the living room; she knew Father probably wanted to talk to me.

After reassuring me that everything would work out well, Father said to pray and meditate only as much as was comfortable for me. He said, "To hold God in your thoughts is as powerful a prayer as you can say." He told me he wanted me to stay in touch with him, until he felt I didn't have to anymore.

"Here is a card with my address and phone number. Write every week or more and call when you feel the need. I want to know how you're doing."

Before Father left, I thanked him for all his help, knelt down and asked his blessing.

When I awoke the next morning, it seemed as if the sun were not shining as brightly as the other days. I didn't feel happy and spirited as I had the day before. I took my time getting ready before going downstairs.

Mrs. Murray was busy creating a bowl of fresh fruit. I was afraid to start up a conversation because I thought I might cry. She must have seen I was worried about something and asked what was wrong. I told her I didn't want to go home because I knew I wasn't wanted there.

"Whoever heard of such a foolish thing?" she said. "Your parents are just as scared as you are. This is a new and different experience for them too. It's your place to help them understand."

Mrs. Murray went on to remind me that I had two sisters and their families were eager to see me. She also emphasized, "Everything will be fine." I gave Mrs. Murray a big hug, and thanked her, knowing she was right. It was time I acted like a 26 year old. Both Mrs. Murray and her daughter made those couple days pleasant and peaceful for me.

Around noon Sandy came. We had lunch. It was time to pack my newly acquired goodies into the car. Hugs and kisses followed and we were off.

It was a 2 1/2 hour ride. We talked a bit, but had long periods of silence. In my mind I was rehearsing what I would say when we reached my home in Milwaukee.

My parents had moved into a small bungalow that I had never seen before. I did know that my dad had a bedroom made out of part of the attic long before they knew I was coming home. We had the address and found it easily.

Sandy followed me up the sidewalk. I rang the doorbell. It felt as if it were forever before my mother came to the door.

I said, "Hi Mom, I'm home." That was the only thing I could think of after all that rehearsing I did in the car. After I stepped into the house, my mother started to close the screen door.

I objected and said, "Let Sandy in, she drove me all this way."

My mother said, "That's not necessary."

I knew my dad was home, so I called, "Daddy, come here." He came. I told him, "I want Sandy to come in because she's my friend and drove me home. Mama doesn't want her to."

Immediately my dad pushed the door open further and said, "Come on in. It was sure nice of you to drive Shirley home."

On our drive down to Milwaukee, I had explained to Sandy that my mother was a little unpredictable, but that she'd like my dad very much. I knew Sandy would understand and not feel offended. After a little light conversation and refreshments, Sandy left.

Chapter Nineteen

It was obvious my parents were at a loss as to what to say to me. I remembered Mrs. Murray saying that it was going to be as difficult for them as it was for me.

I asked, "Did Father call to tell you I was coming home today?"

My mother said, "I had Daddy talk to him, I didn't want to. Are you sure you did the right thing?"

I didn't mention to them at this time that I left without having release papers. All I told them was that Father had taken care of everything. In the eyes of the Vatican I was free to leave. I told them that my decision had not been made in haste. Everything had been done with Father's blessing.

I added, "We'll talk more about this later."

Changing the subject and talking about my parents reversed the atmosphere. My mom suggested I get settled and she would start dinner. My dad was eager to show me the room upstairs that would be mine.

The bedroom had a bed, chest of drawers, a closet and a chair. The room was reminiscent of my convent cell, except there was a mirror. At second glance, I saw the dresser had a doily and some memorabilia from my past. Strange, it was those items that helped me feel at home.

The reunion with my sisters later that evening lightened the situation. At first the conversation was formal, as if they were seeing me as a nun. They were a little put out that they weren't the ones to take me to a restaurant for the first time.

In my own way, I tried to explain to them why I left the convent. I told them the latest Superior brought a great deal of negativity to our convent house. Even though she was never mean to me, I couldn't stand the way some of the other sisters were being treated. I wanted my sisters to realize how rude and belittling that was to those sweet, humble nuns. Using the best words I could think of, I wanted them to understand the superior seemed to do every thing to make the spirit of the house depressing.

My sisters, as well as my parents, found it hard to understand when I told them we were expected to live our vows from our heart as well as outwardly. The ugliness displayed upset me to the point that I couldn't keep my vow of obedience inwardly. I don't think they understood when I told them I felt like a hypocrite wearing the habit. I wanted them to understand that keeping the vows outwardly was easy for me. I felt it was important they know I was considered a good nun. It was hard to admit that inwardly I was bursting to revolt and retaliate for the actions of the Superior.

I mentioned that Reverend Mother did say she would transfer me to a different mission after the school term. It didn't seem to make any difference when I added that my concern was that in years to come this situation could repeat itself and I would be too old to leave.

In a way I believe my parents and sisters really tried to understand. Everything I said to them seemed so foreign. Eventually the conversation turned to the fun we would have getting reacquainted. I was looking forward to seeing my three nephews again. After about ten minutes, a little teasing started. They hadn't forgotten how mischievous I had been growing up. That made it feel a lot like old times. By the time that first day was over, I think my parents, sisters and I were more at ease.

After a week or so, I contacted the education department of the Archdiocese of Milwaukee. I made inquiry to see if there were openings in any of the primary schools for the upcoming semester. I knew contracts had been signed the previous April, but possibly someone had declined. When I realized that was a dead issue, I wrote a letter to Mount Mary College to see about taking a few courses.

Within a couple of days a letter signed by the registrar arrived and I quote:

Dear Miss Gerlach,

   We are sorry but we have a policy that no former member of the Order may study at Mount Mary College. We, therefore, will be unable to accept you as a student for further study.

                              Very sincerely yours,

Needless to say I felt upset and frustrated. I was angry to think I was rejected. Being turned down made me feel as if I were soiled or tarnished. How dare they! All I knew was that I wasn't going to sit around the house. I wanted to do something, but I didn't know what to do.

My dad had an idea for me. He thought it wise to get a job. I didn't have secretarial skills, so he contacted a school that taught the use of a comptometer. Using this machine, a person could add, subtract, multiply and divide rapidly, keeping ones eyes on a list of figures and not on the machine. Being a businessman, my dad knew this skill was an asset in the workplace.

Dad made all the arrangements and paid the tuition after telling me he expected me to pay him back as soon as I had a job. Each student worked the course individually.

I saw to it that I finished the work as quickly as I could. I was the only student there over 19 years of age. I think the other students didn't know what to talk to me about, and I didn't care to talk because I felt so out of place. After four weeks, a job offer came from the Standard Oil Company downtown.

Working at Standard Oil was not a pleasant experience. I had a rude awakening there. About 20 of us were nestled closely together doing the same type of work. There was no conversing during work time, but we shared the same morning and afternoon break, as well as lunchtime. It became apparent from the very beginning that the workers formed two groups. The one group was very critical of everything the other group said, how they looked and dressed, and how little work they were doing. Interestingly, the other group thought and felt the same about the first group.

I had no idea that such pettiness existed among adults. I refused to be a part of either group; so therefore, I spent a great deal of time alone. My dad reminded me that I needed a job, so I was to ignore the situation and do my work well. My mother was sure that I had done something to divide the workers.

All this while, I continued to be in touch with Father, as he had requested. I wrote letters frequently and called him on occasion. He heard all my stories of how strained my relationship was with my parents. Not only was it difficult for them to have me in their house that was built for two, but I felt uneasy there also.

It seemed that whatever I did was wrong. I spoke too much; I spoke too little. I found it difficult to understand why they were doing some things the way they did. Also, it was obvious I was still a 16- year- old to them. I knew I was getting on their nerves as much as they were on mine. I explained to Father that I was trying to accommodate my parents, but it was like walking on eggs.

It's difficult to explain, but one of the things that bothered them most was the fact that I said please and thank you all the time. It had just become a way of life for me in the convent. If at the table, I would say, "Please pass the butter" or "Thank you, Mama" when she ironed a blouse for me or brought me a soft drink, my words upset her very much.

Both parents chastised me. They seemed to take turns saying things like, "We don't talk like that. We just do things. Stop saying that please and thank you all the time." One day Dad asked if I was trying to upset my mother.

There was no hesitation on my part to tell Father also my tales of woe regarding my job. He laughed when I mentioned the two factions at work.

He said. "Welcome to the world we live in." I remember interjecting it was just foolish gossip they were indulging in and not meanness as I had seen previously.

Father said, "Don't stoop to the level of others. Set your standards and live by them."

I was still a fish out of water in my new world.

My sisters and parents introduced me to plenty of new experiences. It had been ten and a half years since I had walked into large public places. I remember only too well walking into a large grocery store for the first time after leaving the convent. The sight and smell of all that food overwhelmed me and I instantly became ill.

Growing up, I never noticed a peculiar mixture of smell from food, cartons and people in large grocery stores. No matter how great the ventilation system was that day, it really hit me. My stomach felt as if it was upside down and I became lightheaded. Immediate fresh air was the only solution.

Drive-in theaters were the rage at that time. Whoever heard of sitting out in the open air and watching a movie? I learned how to stand in line at the concession stand. I found out there is an art to holding your place in line and not letting anyone move ahead of you. If you weren't fast enough getting in line, the intermission was never long enough. It was fun. I had forgotten what it was like to be out at night.

Over the next couple weeks, one by one relatives started stopping in at our house. I felt as if I were an exhibition or display. They were polite enough, but it was obvious they watched whatever I did. They took note of my hair, the fact that I wore lipstick and special note when I crossed my legs. They knew nuns never crossed their legs in public.

It made me smile inside as they struggled for small talk. Eyebrows were raised if I drank a glass of beer.

My parents were uncomfortable, probably apprehensive as to what I might say or do. Sometimes they would steer the conversation if it came close to my being asked about what went on in the convent. It was awkward to say the least.

In my heart I knew the company wanted to know if I did something inappropriate and as a result had been asked to leave the convent. Avoiding any particulars became a game for me. There seemed no reason to continue to hash over what had transpired in the convent house. I wasn't comfortable talking about the superior and her actions. I felt I owed my family an explanation, but it wasn't anyone else's business. I chose to leave and now I was home.

After being home a couple months, a postcard came in the mail addressed to me. The message read, as best I remember, that I was to present myself at the Motherhouse on a certain Saturday, at such and such a time, to sign my release papers. I was never asked if that date or time was agreeable.

Actually, I didn't feel the need to sign any papers; the permission of the Vatican was enough for me. My parents thought my coming home wouldn't be legal in the eyes of the church unless I signed them.

I begged my dad to go with me, but he refused. Dad was a convert to Catholicism and was only comfortable with our parish priest. Other priests and nuns intimidated him, I believe.

Because I didn't know how to drive, I took the bus to downtown Milwaukee and eventually found my way to the Motherhouse. After ringing the doorbell at the front entrance, I was ushered into a small parlor by the portress sister.

All she said was, "Someone will attend you shortly." After a while, a tall, stately, formidable, non-smiling sister entered the room and laid some papers on a table. I recognized her as one of the members of the Provincialate.

After I said, "Hello Sister," she ruffled through the papers, handed me a pen and said, "Sign here and here."

Stunned, I did just that. I signed and signed.

After that, she stood erect, crossed her arms in her big sleeves, focused her eyes directly on me and said, "You know you've turned your back on God. Shame on you!"

She continued by saying she hoped I realized that someday I would go insane. She added that any children born to me would be crippled or maimed. She emphasized that I would probably be a slave to alcohol. She added, there would be no happiness in my life and that she had pity on my soul.

Sister turned and gathered up her papers as she floated out the room. I was devastated. All I could think of was that Father would say she's wrong. I wondered if she thought of herself or the Order as a failure because of me. Maybe that's why she said those things. I wondered if words of that sort were said to everyone that left.

I sat down in a chair. I don't know why I did that, because there was nothing to wait for. After a few minutes I got up and left again through the front door.

When I returned home, I told my parents I signed the papers; but I never had the heart to tell them what Sister had said. They probably would have believed her.

Later I realized I should have asked for a copy of the papers. I'm sure there was one for me. If I had been more experienced and not so naïve, I probably would've handled all that differently.

Chapter Twenty

In the beginning of 1952, almost six months after I returned home, I took the train to the Valley in order to visit with Father. We had a long conversation. He told me he believed it was in my best interest to leave home. He said it was obvious to him that I would never get on with my life under my parents' roof. This startled me.

I explained to Father that my mother and I were just beginning to be comfortable with one another again. I think my dad found it easier to get along with my mother when I was there. I felt I brought so much difficulty to my parents having left home and then asking them to take me back. I believed leaving now would be out of the question.

Father saw things differently. I wasn't looking for a social life, but Father felt it was important. He explained that living with my parents precluded this from ever happening. I explained that I didn't want a relationship; in fact the thought of it scared me terribly. Father said I needed to take responsibility for my life -- to be on my own. His next suggestion blew me away.

Without hesitation he said, "Shirley, I want you to move back to the Fox River Valley."

"That's out of the question Father, I can't come back here. People will know me. I've had so many children under my care over the years and became well acquainted with their parents. They'll recognize me."

As I expected, Father said, "Now, now, everything will be just fine." He went on to explain that it was important for the laity to mingle with someone who has left the convent and has remained principled.

"I know they'll welcome you whole heartedly. Take my word for it," he said.

I knew Father had been guiding me well, but I felt this was too much to ask of me. I told him I only wanted to live a quiet life. I anticipated getting a better job and not having to rely on my parents.

"You told me you wanted to live your life for God. You're not going to hide your light under the roof of a bungalow. Now, here's my plan," he said.

I took a deep breath and said to myself, *What's coming now?*

Father told me they were hiring at the Marathon Corporation and he was sure they would have something I could do. He had checked with Mrs. Murray and she told Father she would be pleased to rent a room to me. He went on to say that before the end of the year, he was sure I'd be able to afford my own apartment.

"Tomorrow give notice at Standard Oil that you'll be leaving. Be sure to tell your parents and family that you'll be working at Marathon Corporation and living at Mrs. Murray's house." He added, "Invite them to come when you do and they'll see you'll have a nice place to live."

"Father, what if I can't do the work at Marathon?"

"Their accounting offices are so big there certainly is a job that you can do. I checked and they are hiring." He kept assuring me that everything would be fine.

Father said I was to take the train up to the Valley the following Friday. He reminded me that Marathon Corporation was in walking distance from the station. He said to go to personnel and ask for an application. "They'll be nice to you there, I know," he added.

My head was spinning and my stomach was churning. I knew Father had guided me through this whole process. I don't know what I would have done without his help. Something inside of me told me to continue to trust him. I wondered though if he really knew how difficult it was going to be for me to tell my parents.

Before our conversation was over, Father told me to stop at the rectory the following Friday to see him, after I had been to the personnel office. He said he wanted to hear how I handled telling my parents and family about the move.

When Father offered to drive me to the train station, he said we'd stop at Mrs. Murray's first.

"She'll be glad to see you," he said. He went on to tell me that I probably would like to hear from her that I was welcome to stay with her.

Nothing had changed. Mrs. Murray was as sweet and hospitable as she had been before. I think she knew we'd stop by, because she had coffee and desserts ready. She told me she was eager for me to come and live with her. She said I could have free run of the kitchen and would be pleased to have me share any meals with her. After a short visit we were off to the train station and I was on my way home to face my parents.

During the train ride home, my mind was in constant turmoil. What had I gotten myself into? Just changing jobs can be traumatic. I was going to quit my job, tell my parents I was moving to another city, and then actually move without a job lined up. That sure didn't sound stable to me.

Would it be wise to quit my job and then come home and tell my parents what I did? They're going to ask me what Father had to say. I'll have to tell them something. The only alternative I had was to make a clean breast of everything.

The bus ride from the train station to my home was progressing too quickly. I felt fortunate when I saw a couple of cars parked in front of my parents' home. Thank God for company!

After exchanging greetings with everyone and responding that I had a very nice time visiting with a friend, I excused myself and went to my room. When I heard the company leave, I went downstairs to face the music.

Reluctantly I joined my parents in the living room and said, "I have something to tell you."

As calmly as I could, I told them about moving, renting a room from Mrs. Murray, and anticipating a job at the Marathon Corporation. While I was on a roll, I added that I was giving notice the next day at Standard Oil and taking the train again to the Valley on

Friday to fill out an application. I stressed that Father said he was sure there would be some kind of a job available for me.

The floodgates opened! My mother began to cry. Her expression was a combination of anger and that of a victim. Her concern was not so much my leaving home, but the fact, as she put it, "Only bad girls leave home."

In the early fifties, it was common for an unwed mother-to-be to be sent out of town to have the baby. My mother couldn't understand. "Why are you doing this to me?" she cried. My dad tried to calm her down. I felt horrible; no way did I want to hurt my parents.

My dad said he thought we were getting along all right the way we were, but added he knew I should get on with my life. I think my dad felt that Father's judgment was sound.

From the beginning, Dad had been pleased about the way Father took good care of me through the whole process of leaving the convent.

The rest of the week we didn't talk much about the big change, except that my folks asked if I gave notice at my job on Monday. The talk with my immediate boss and supervisor all went smoothly. Management at Standard Oil was satisfied if I stayed through Thursday, because I had already asked to have off on Friday.

During the week my dad took me aside and suggested that if I was determined to go, it would be best that I make the move this Friday instead of dragging it all out another week. He felt it would be easier on my mother.

Dad said he would pay Mrs. Murray my first month's rent. Surely I would have some kind of a job before the month was over. He suggested I call Mrs. Murray to see if the early move would be fine with her. Dad also thought we should keep Father aware of our intended early move.

I don't think my sisters thought my new plan a good idea. They knew when I was in the convent I had to go where my assignment took me. Now that I was free to make my own choice, I don't think they understood why I would choose to live away from Milwaukee. It was hard to explain that Father thought it best for me to be totally on my own.

I knew that even if I had my own apartment in Milwaukee, I'd have been content to center my life around my sisters' families and my parents. This is why I think Father felt I had to make a clean break and test my wings. The more I thought about it, the more I knew Father was right.

Friday morning my dad drove me and my few belongings to my new home. My Mother chose not to join us. Dad and I had a nice talk in the car on the way up. I felt he was a mixture of glad and sad. He told me he would miss me and that he liked having me home again. I think also, he was a little excited for me because he kept assuring me that being on one's own was an exhilarating experience.

When we arrived and before we got out of the car, Dad gave me some money and said, "Here, you don't want to have to ask for anything."

I could tell from the start that Dad liked Mrs. Murray. They exchanged easy chatter and each made the other laugh. When we took my things upstairs, he commented that he knew I'd be happy there.

After checking out the view, we went downstairs and enjoyed the meal Mrs. Murray had prepared. The conversation was light and cheerful. I could tell Dad was pleased with this whole arrangement. I had previously asked him if he would like to meet Father. I knew Father would have been pleased to meet him. Dad declined, but said he appreciated my asking.

Before leaving for home, Dad drove me to the personnel office to complete the application process at the Marathon Corporation. I thanked Dad for bringing me to my new home and making it so pleasant for me. He gave me as big a hug as I gave him. I told him I loved him and that he was very special to me. When saying goodbye, I promised to write and call frequently.

That feeling of aloneness crept over me as I watched Dad drive away. I asked myself, "How many new beginnings do I have to make?"

It was easy to find the personnel office. I walked over to the woman at the information desk and said, "May I please have a job application?" She asked my name.

As soon as I said, "I'm Shirley Gerlach," that's as far as I got. The woman flipped open a folder and said, "Hi Shirley, sign here. Are you able to start on Monday?" This took my breath away. Father had arranged all of this. No wonder he was so sure there would be a job for me.

The young woman went on to explain that at this location there were two plants. Even though each plant had its own accounting office, there was a combined

office called central accounting. She suggested that I
come to her office on Monday morning so she could
take me to central accounting to meet my boss. And
that was it. Father couldn't have made it easier for me.

On leaving there, I took a cab to the rectory of
Father's parish. He was pleased it all went as smoothly
as he had planned. We talked about my leaving home,
and my dad bringing me to Mrs. Murray's.

My biggest concern still was what I was going to do
when I met the fathers of my former students.
Marathon was in the same town in which I taught
school. I asked Father if this new boss already knew I
was an ex-nun. Reluctantly Father said he did and that
my coworkers also knew about my coming. It was
obvious the woman in personnel must have known as
well, because she was overly attentive and
exceptionally gracious with me.

I kept asking Father, "How can I possibly look these
people in the face? This is just not going to work."

Father sat upright in his chair, looked me straight in
the eyes and said, "You have done nothing wrong. I
expect you to walk into that office with your head held
high, a smile on your face and with an attitude of
wanting to get to work."

I was waiting for Father to add, "Everything will be
fine."

Having Father's help was like having my own
guardian angel on earth. In my heart I knew I had done
the right thing and God was providing the guidance I
needed. I was blessed indeed.

The days went by quickly. I was having fun living
with Mrs. Murray. I didn't miss the strain of the

parent/child relationship that I had in Milwaukee. I was very happy.

On Saturday, Sandy and her twelve year old son stopped by. I heard Mrs. Murray greeting them. My heart skipped a beat as I pictured this lad seeing me as a layperson for the first time.

Mrs. Murray called up the stairs, "Shirley, we have company. Come on down."

I remembered Father's statement about holding my head up high. I walked down the steps and said, "Hi Sandy. Hello Eric."

To my amazement, everything was fine.

Eric walked over to me, smiled, shook my hand as his mother must have suggested and said, "Hi, it's nice to see you."

I was so pleased. I wanted to hug him. The four of us visited and later played a game while enjoying Mrs. Murray's treats. It turned out to be a fun day. Something told me it wasn't going to be so bad meeting the fathers working at Marathon.

Before I knew it, it was Monday. I was able to walk to work comfortably. By this time I had enough experience walking with a two-inch heel. No more low-heeled shoes for me.

As I entered the personnel office, the same woman I had spoken to on Friday walked up to me and introduced herself as Ruth. She took me to the central accounting office and introduced me to the man who would be my boss for the next couple of years. I had had his son in sixth grade.

Mike seemed comfortable calling me Shirley and me using his first name. He took time to explain about the function of central accounting and some of my responsibilities. As a boss, Mike was a pleasant contrast from the people I had to deal with at Standard Oil.

Out of the next 15 individuals I was introduced to, I recognized at least a dozen of them. Each one greeted me as one would a new employee, and no one mentioned the convent. I breathed a sigh of relief and was eager to start working.

At work, I was assigned a variety of jobs to do and enjoyed every one of them. I was grateful no typing was required. Being familiar working with numbers, it appeared that as long as I kept my mind on what I was doing, this was a perfect job for me. Everyday at the office was like a new challenge.

It was taken for granted that everyone was on a first name basis in the office. Having known most of my coworkers as Mr. or Mrs. when I was teaching, it was awkward to say their first names. I couldn't help but notice some weren't at ease saying Shirley either.

After some weeks, I started receiving weekend dinner invitations to the home of several of the coworkers who I had known before. Somehow they would always work it into the conversation that their spouse was very eager to see me also. I know they were being very kind and generous, but in my heart I was sure there was a little curiosity connected to the offer. The wives probably wondered what I looked like out of the habit.

In the beginning I would dream up little excuses for not going. Finally I realized they were not going to let up, so I acquiesced. They always offered to pick me up at my house. I lived in the same neighboring town as Father did, so it would have been too far to walk to their homes. For quite a while I had a place to go every Saturday and Sunday.

By going to the various homes, I found myself being with the youngsters who had been my students. One student, who now lives in Illinois, still keeps in touch with me after some 55 years. I was his teacher in second, third and sixth grade. He frequently reminds me of projects we did and the fun we had.

Meeting the families wasn't as difficult as I anticipated. What helped I think, was that the parents didn't treat me as an ex-teacher or ex-nun visiting, but rather just as a new friend. Several of the families remained good friends all the while I lived in the Valley.

We all know people who enjoy the role of matchmaker. By the second time I visited some of these homes, an older son, a nephew or a very dear friend of theirs just happened to be over too.

Some excuse was always made so that we would be alone in the same room for a while. I knew what my hosts had planned. This made me feel very awkward and uneasy. All of this was so new to me, I didn't know how to act or carry on a conversation.

Invariably the man would ask if I cared to see a movie, some art display or theater presentation. And then too, I found out that some just wanted to go to a bar and hang out.

I was never comfortable being with any of these men. It seemed they couldn't carry on an interesting conversation. I don't think they were looking for conversation.

A few of them were downright odd, like the one who had a fetish for hygiene, I think. He wore gloves all the time. I noticed a reluctance on his part to even take them off in a restaurant. He told me that sometimes he liked to bring his own silverware to where he was eating.

I dated another fellow whose mother I knew quite well. It makes me laugh now to remember that I threatened to tell on him to his mother about his offensive actions and foul language. It was very difficult to have an intelligent conversation with most of these men. After a few of these dates, it was pretty easy for me to see why these guys needed someone to set them up.

Father was still keeping tabs on me, so I spoke to him rather frequently. He was always interested to know what was going on at work. I told him about these visits to the various homes and of course meeting these available men. He had very strong opinions about some of them.

After I went on a date, Father questioned me somewhat and then invariably said, "Don't see that one again". I don't think I ever saw any of these men more than twice. After the second date, Father would say, "No, no, not for you."

I never minded Father's questions. I treasured the thought that someone really cared what happened to me. Actually I really wasn't looking for a relationship. That never crossed my mind even when I was considering leaving the convent.

Chapter Twenty-one

When spring came, Mrs. Murray's daughter, Şandy, thought I ought to learn to drive. She and her husband would ask me over for dinner frequently. It turned out they became great friends of mine.

Bill took me out to drive in the afternoon after I got my temporary license. That didn't last too long because he said I made him nervous. I didn't tell him, but he made me nervous too.

Sandy started to drive with me on a regular basis. After a while she went with me to take the behind the wheel test. I didn't have a car but at least now I could drive.

After a couple of months, it was they who helped me find an apartment. I bought a bed, a sofa, and an easy chair. The table and chair set I bought had to be assembled and finished. Even though Bill did all the assembling, Sandy and I kept giving him directions until he asked us to leave him alone.

We all worked on the finishing of the tables and chairs. I don't think any of us had experience with that before, so it was quite a project. We did make a unanimous decision never to again buy furniture that wasn't stained and varnished. In spite of our mishaps and mess, it was great fun.

Sandy and Bill introduced me to many new people outside the office. If they went to a concert, or to hear a new music group, they always took me along. We developed a tradition of going to a movie every Sunday night and then stopping for a couple beers.

Sandy saw to it that I took golf lessons. Frequently after work, she and a couple of friends would pick me up to go golfing. They were most patient with me as I went from sand trap to sand trap. After many lessons and much practice, it wasn't I who held up the foursome. I was so excited about having fun in my life.

Bill and their son Eric were good tennis players. Eric did his best to teach me to play. It wasn't too long after that that we agreed I made a better spectator than player.

When Mrs. Murray's family had a get-together, Bill and Sandy picked me up on the way. I was always included.

During the summer the three accounting offices had a combined picnic at a beautiful park. We gathered in the afternoon for games and foolishness. There was a mountain of food to be consumed and the liquid refreshment was basically beer and soda.

At dusk the mosquitoes drove us into the clubhouse. Some people sat around and talked, others played cards and the rest just kept mingling and enjoying one another's company. Every so often a tune coming from the jukebox would prompt some to get up and dance. I think I enjoyed dancing more than anyone else.

*   *   *

As a youngster I loved to dance. On occasion in the convent during recreation, our Superior would play some phonograph records. When a waltz, fox trot or two-step was played, it wasn't hard to find a partner to dance.

During the holidays when we had longer recreation, we would go over to the library in school and put records on the phonograph in order to dance. Many sisters were better dancers than I.

*   *   *

During the course of the evening at the picnic, Art and Les, each the head of the two other accounting sections, made it their mission to see that I met everyone at the picnic. I recall meeting a young man by the name of Jim. He worked in Art's accounting office. I think I danced with him once, but didn't see him the rest of the evening. I wasn't impressed.

In the weeks following the picnic, this same young man, Jim, often found himself at my desk when he came to central accounting. Somehow or other, he'd start a conversation with me. He was very handsome and pleasant; I didn't mind at all.

It so happened that when something needed to be dropped off in Jim's accounting department, I was sure to volunteer. I saw to it that my walk would take me past Jim's desk too, and there was always time for a little chat.

Sometime later Jim asked if I cared to have lunch with him on a Friday. Needless to say I said yes. We had many of these lunches together. I thought this lunch business was never going to end. I was waiting for him to ask me on a date. It took some time before he finally asked me out.

One day Jim asked if I had ever been to a stock car race. I hadn't, so he explained what it was. He told me there was a racetrack near his sister's house and he'd like to take me there. This was our first evening date.

Jim came to the door to pick me up and we went down a flight of stairs to the parking lot. As he walked to the driver's side of the car, he said, "You look like a healthy girl, you can handle the door on your side".

I was taken a back, but decided to make nothing of the fact that on a date, I expected my door to be opened for me.

The times we went to lunch, I automatically opened the car door and got in. The fact that Jim made the remark told me, he knew I expected him to handle the door. After all, this was a real date. Time proved that Jim's openness and straightforward manner was just one of his many charms.

It turned out the racetrack was crude and very dusty. Every time the cars went whizzing by, they threw up mounds of dust. Not only were we covered with it, but from cheering the drivers on, we tasted it also. I didn't mind, I was having a great time being with Jim.

On the way home we stopped for a couple of beers and we talked for several hours. I was so impressed. From our conversation I concluded Jim was the first man I met who was intelligent, humorous and respectful. The old cliché, "tall, dark and handsome," describes well this 6-foot man with beautiful dark hair and handsome features.

Jim had enlisted in the Army during World War II. He signed up for the Reserves and was recalled during the Korean conflict. He had just returned from active duty when I met him in 1952. Marathon Corporation had held his job while he was in service.

During our lunches on Fridays, Jim's and my conversation had been pretty much about work, my learning to play golf and even the weather. Prior to this night I had dodged going into detail about my time before I started at the Marathon Corporation. Jim knew I was from Milwaukee and before working at Standard Oil, I taught grade school.

That night I knew it was time to fess up and explain about my being in the convent. To my surprise, he had already heard about that from someone at the office. He knew nothing of my experience, but said he figured I'd get around to telling him when I was ready.

Our evening dates were few and far between in the beginning. Gradually our Friday lunches expanded to lunch during the week. Sometimes I packed a lunch or we'd stop and pick up something before driving to a nearby park. I looked forward to being with him more and more.

Jim was only two years older than I, but I was taken with the fact that not only was he handsome and fun to be with, he was serious about completing his education and improving himself. Something was telling me inside that I wanted to see a lot of him.

Jim came from a family of ten children. His parents were deceased when I met him. Gradually he introduced me to his brothers' and sisters' families. I loved meeting so many new people with many different occupations and interests. They seemed to be

as comfortable with me as I was with them. They liked
to play cards as much as I, which added to my
pleasure.

I kept Father posted with what I was doing and with
whom I was spending time. I told him about seeing Jim
and he never said not to. I let Father know I liked Jim
more than anybody else I had met.

The time came when I wanted Jim to meet my
family. I worked up courage to call home to tell my
parents I had met a man I wanted them to meet. I didn't
go into any great detail on the phone, because I didn't
want my mother to ask questions about Jim.

There was one commandment about marriage that
my mother held dear. She told each of her daughters,
"See that you marry a rich man and not an Irishman."
No way did I want to explain over the phone that Jim
was not rich, and that he was a full blooded Irishman.
After conferring with my dad, my mother said the
following Sunday would be fine. She said she'd have
dinner ready by noon and we were not to be late.

We gauged our drive to Milwaukee to ensure our
prompt arrival at noon. Jim stopped and picked up
some flowers for my mom. She accepted the flowers
graciously as we went through the introductions.

My mom set out some hors d'oeuvres before she
went back to the kitchen for last-minute dinner
preparation. I could tell my dad had paved the way for
us. We were off to a good start.

Jim and my dad found many things to talk about.
When politics was discussed, they had many opinions
in common. The conversation floated from politics to
business, and then to politics again. I could tell from

the start that my dad liked Jim. They were on a first name basis by the time Mom said dinner was ready.

I had rejoined the men in the living room after making a polite offer to help my mom in the kitchen. I knew she would reject the offer, but I felt it appropriate at least to make the gesture.

Jim was convinced my mother was the best cook he had ever met. I think he raved about every dish she set before us. My mom didn't have anything negative to say about Jim. After all, he passed the test with flying colors when he praised her cooking. I was so relieved because we had a very pleasant visit.

One weekend my parents came to spend time with me at my apartment. I was a nervous wreck before they ever arrived. I could hear my mother comment on the fact that I only had a sofa and a small table with four chairs in the living room. The table and chairs were in the middle of the room, the sofa to the left and an artificial plant on the right to balance the room.

I dreaded the fact that I had to show my folks the bedroom, because there was absolutely nothing else in the room other than the bed. There were a couple shelves in the closet that I used as a dresser. I knew my dad wouldn't care, but I was convinced my mom would have a great deal to say about the apartment. The kitchen was very tiny, but it did have a stove and refrigerator.

Watching for their car, I saw them drive into the parking lot. I went downstairs to greet them. The apartment was upstairs from a store with high ceilings, so the stairway was rather long to the upper level. They managed to catch their breath before we went into the living room.

I had to chuckle to myself when Dad walked into the living room and said, "Nice and airy. It's really nice and airy."

Mom's lips were tight together. I knew she was thinking a lot, but probably had been told not to say too much. The only thing I recall her saying when we went into the bedroom was, "Girl, how can you live like this?"

I reassured her I was very happy the way things were.

We sat in the living room and visited a bit. My mother saw I had the table set for four. She asked if we were waiting for Jim. I assured her that he would be there shortly. Mom brought up the fact that Jim was late. She wondered if he didn't know they were coming.

I tried to explain that certainly something must have happened to delay him. Actually I was not too happy about his being late also. I remember going to the kitchen and checking on the food a couple of times.

No one was happier than I when the doorbell rang. After Jim arrived, my mother was appeased because he was very charming with her.

I remember feeling very awkward serving the dinner; what was served I don't recall. The only thing that could be said about the meal was that it was edible. I do know I felt a great sense of relief when the table was cleared.

Jim suggested that he take us for a ride. We showed them the church that I attended in Neenah before driving to the Marathon Corporation in Menasha. Jim explained all about the carton and paraffin plants, along with the three different accounting offices.

From there we drove to Appleton to see St. Mary's, the church that Jim attended. We also went past the house he was living in with his sister. From there we drove around several of the lakes in the area.

I felt emotionally exhausted when my folks finally took off for Milwaukee. The day went fairly well. I had imagined the worst, but it didn't happen. I didn't make a big impression on them with my cooking. Since cooking was my mother's strength, I wasn't a threat to her. Nothing provoked arguments or emotional upheavals.

I think it was important for my folks to see me in my own surroundings, settled and happy. I recall that was the time I realized my parents no longer thought of me as a teenager, but as a grown woman.

Sometime later, Jim and I drove to Milwaukee again. My mother made a wonderful meal that we shared with my sisters and their families. We all went bowling and had a great time.

I took particular note of how well Jim interacted with my nephews. My thought was that if we were to ever marry, he would be good with children.

A week or so before Easter in 1954, I told Father that I thought I was in love with Jim. I had a hunch with the approaching holiday Jim was going to ask me to marry him.

When discussing this with Father, he didn't say that he approved or disapproved of a marriage. He maintained the attitude of let's just wait and see.

His only comment was, "You'll know what to do."

I didn't know how to read his being so noncommittal. Prior to this, Father always had a definite response of yes or no about everything.

The Saturday night before Easter, Jim and I had a date with another couple to go out to dinner. At one point while the other couple was dancing, Jim proposed and gave me a diamond ring. I guess with or without Father, I wanted to say yes and I did.

In my heart I knew I wanted to live the rest of my life with Jim. There was no doubt in my mind that he would take good care of me. He was a man of integrity with mental and physical strength. I couldn't wait to call my folks with my news.

On their return to the table, I found out the other couple knew Jim's intention all along.

We had a good laugh over the fact that they wondered how often they would have to dance before Jim got up the nerve to ask me.

Following Easter Sunday Mass, I waited for an appropriate time before going to see Father in a small room behind the altar called the sacristy.

I came into the sacristy saying, "Look, look what I have!" as I showed him the ring. I quickly told Father that Jim had proposed and I said yes.

Father didn't seem to be surprised at all. He just smiled as he looked at the ring.

I went on to say that we were thinking of a September wedding. I asked if he would be willing to officiate even if we'd be married at St. Mary's in Appleton, which was not his parish.

Father asked me to sit down. He told me how beautiful the ring was, but said he would not officiate, nor would he attend the wedding.

I couldn't believe my ears.

I said, "Father, why are you talking like this? You have been like a Guardian Angel for me these past few years. You helped me over all the rough spots. You cared about me. What would've happened to me without you? You don't mean this."

Father smiled. He told me it was very kind of me to say what I did, but he said he was only doing his work. He explained that there were many people he was working with. He added that his mission in life was to be of service. In a slow emphatic way Father said I was never to call him again or to visit him again.

I was on the verge of tears when I said, "Father, what are you doing to me? You've been like a father to me. Are you upset because I accepted Jim's proposal?"

"Now, now," he said, "You know me better than that. Don't you think I would have said something before this if I disapproved of Jim?"

Father repeated that there are other people to help and that I was ready to move ahead without him. Seeing that I was upset, Father reminded me that it was very important in religious life not to become attached to any person. He said marriage is a relationship of two and that I was to build my life now with my husband.

Father stood and so did I. He took my hands in his and as he looked me straight in the eyes and said, "I know you'll be just fine in the hands of that big Irishman."

Epilogue

Shirley and Jim married in 1954, and they spent the next fifty-four years raising a family and building a successful and exciting life. Shirley continued to teach elementary school and later became Jim's business partner and right arm, supporting him through a 28-year political career in the City of Milwaukee.

Shirley once said, "I've really had a wonderful and fascinating life. Being in the convent gave me the opportunity to learn that I had potential, and it gave me discipline. With Jim's career, I had exciting opportunities, ate dinner with two US presidents and met the Pope. We were blessed with six healthy children and traveled to six continents."

Even through life's most difficult challenges, Shirley never wavered in her love for and faith in God. Her youngest son died in 1967 in a tragic accident. Her 23-year old son died in an automobile crash in 1979, and she lost her 41-year old daughter to cancer in 2002. These experiences planted her even more firmly in her lifelong quest for spirituality and truth, which manifested through a variety of universal and metaphysical pursuits.

Shirley studied and eventually taught classes in the ancient wisdoms, astrology and numerology. She founded Mind Spirit Institute in Milwaukee, where she practiced clinical hypnotherapy for over ten years until she retired. She was a respected teacher and counselor, whose genuine caring helped countless others in both small and significant ways.

Shirley passed away on July 5, 2011 at the age of 85, before she was able to see this memoir published. Those who were fortunate enough to be touched by and to love this remarkable woman will always treasure her life, love, counsel, and memories.

Made in the USA
Lexington, KY
01 February 2012